to pursuing one's own peace and identity, *Shift Your Thinking* offers jewels of wisdom that engage and inspire us to shift our thinking and step into lives of greater significance and satisfaction."

—**Helen Steinkamp**, cofounder of Marketplace Women

"As a cogent and original transformational work, *Shift Your Thinking* offers strategic approaches for adapting to an epic shift in the way we think and feel about ourselves, about our jobs, about the way we live life and express ourselves in relationship, and about what horizon we call destiny. The wisdom in this book is timeless and a must-read for anybody committed to ordering the chaos of life and releasing beauty."

—**Daniel L. Tocchini**, author of *Us* and *In the Twinkle of an "I"*

"Whether in person or through the written word, Dean has a way of getting to the heart of the matter . . . that is, *your* heart. His selections are quick and easy to read but not to be mistaken for simple. He layers meaning in a way that delivers impact long past the initial reading."

—**Alynne Mann Golding**, CEO of TrendSpotters

"Occasionally a book comes along that drives you to reflect on the important things in life, and delivers truth in a way that makes the investment of time well worth the read. With certainty, *Shift Your Thinking* will help improve your life page by page. It's a book you can give to anyone, and they won't just thank you for the gift, they'll thank you for helping them improve their life. It's that compelling."

—**Dr. Jim Masteller**, founder and CEO of The Center for Individual and Family Therapy; retired US Army chaplain

"*Shift Your Thinking* is thought provoking and appeals to the soul. Pulling at the corners of your mind, this artful composition causes questions to rise and fall as you read one and then another of these tantalizing short essays on life and all its complexities. If you or someone you know wants to transform from ordinary to extraordinary, this book will help!"

—**Beth Ganem**, CEO of the Ganem Group

"*Shift Your Thinking* is an anthology of thought-provoking, digestible insights into fundamental principles of success in many facets of life. *Shift Your Thinking* will jolt your mind into new pathways of thought."

—**Jerrell Shelton**, retired CEO of Thomson Reuters
Business Information Group

"*Shift Your Thinking* pays particular homage to the age-old wisdom that 'words are fingers that mold the mind.' Del Sesto has captured essential and transformational messages to help each and every one of us better steer our ship during the course of our life. It is a must-read."

—**Ralph Adamo**, president and
CEO of Integrity Wealth Management

"*Shift Your Thinking* is not only a book that people will read and share, it is also likely to become a mission they will embrace. In my opinion, it is one of the more meaningful gifts you ever could give to yourself and to others."

—**Dave Dias**, vice president of InterWest;
author of *Sales Ethos: Building Long Term Client Value*

"Dean Del Sesto writes the way he talks, with clarity, incisiveness, and discernment. While reading *Shift Your Thinking*, I braced myself because I knew that whatever Dean has to say would feel like it was directed precisely at me. It's as if he reads my mind page by page, taking sharp aim and giving me a compelling case for changing my thinking, my actions, or my attitude. *Shift Your Thinking* will lock onto your mind and won't let go, so reader, be forewarned: growing isn't optional."

—**Shelley Leith**, coauthor of *Character Makeover*;
developer of the 40 Days of Purpose Campaign

"Like proverbs for the modern (and postmodern) soul, Dean Del Sesto's bite-size wisdom punches where it matters most and releases deeply over time. These words will be a gift to you. That is, of course, if you don't miss them."

—**Dane Sanders**, author of *Fast Track Photographer*
and *The Fast Track Photographer Business Plan*

"Never boring and always inspiring, *Shift Your Thinking* has become a part of our corporate culture. Unlike most books that focus just on a singular topic, *Shift Your Thinking* is an intelligent convergence of many topics to help build a better person in all aspects of life. This book will build a stronger, more relational, higher-performing culture in any company that chooses to provide it to its employees. From entry level to the C-level, *Shift Your Thinking* is relevant to everyone."

—**Brian Fischbein**, CEO of Crescent Solutions, Inc.

"You'll quickly realize in reading *Shift Your Thinking* that Dean is a gifted wordsmith. But before putting it on paper so eloquently, he is first a gifted thinker, looking at everything in an innovative, disruptive, challenging way. Savor this gem just one page at a time, and walk away each day with unforgettable perspectives that will have you marinating on his insights until you embrace the next page the next day."

—**Rick McCarthy**, CEO of McCarthy CPAs

"*Shift Your Thinking* is insightful, thought provoking, and challenging. As one who walks his talk, Dean is able to engage our minds and hearts on topics that really matter and help us focus on taking action to improve our character and life. Read, engage, and grow!"

—**Chris Duncan**, CEO of SimplyWin

"Dean Del Sesto uses words, almost surgically, to amplify life's issues, reveal life's misconceptions, and gift the reader with a better understanding of how to maximize life. *Shift Your Thinking* will move you to take action and will grow your frame of reference into new territory."

—**Sanford Coggins**, CEO of VisionWise
Capital Management

"So many books offer the empty promise that they will 'change your life.' However, if there was one book I could recommend that has the potential to be life changing, it would be *Shift Your Thinking*. If you are content with your life being the same tomorrow as it is today, then perhaps this isn't the book for you, because *Shift Your Thinking* will challenge you to rethink and reshape your life in just about every area."

—**William Jordan**, president of WJA; author of
Strategic Wealth and *The Seven Percent Solution*

"Truth changes you, if you're willing to interact with it. Unfortunately, these days truth is hard to find in the mess and quantity of information that hits us daily. In *Shift Your Thinking*, Dean has taken truths that have a unique way of cutting straight to the core and packaged them in manageable bites. These bites have incredible power in the way they speak to your soul and push you to action, one step at a time. Read it, share it, and live it. You'll be glad you did!"

—**Gary Sikes**, president and CEO of Elevation

SHIFT YOUR THINKING

200 WAYS
TO IMPROVE YOUR LIFE

DEAN DEL SESTO

© 2013 by Dean Del Sesto

Published by Revell
a division of Baker Publishing Group
P.O. Box 6287, Grand Rapids, MI 49516-6287
www.revellbooks.com

Spire edition published 2016

ISBN 978-0-8007-2687-4

Previously published in 2013 under the title *ShiftPoints*

Printed in the United States of America

16   17   18   19   20   21   22   8   7   6   5

Acknowledgments

There are so many people who have impacted my life and my heart to write this book. First and foremost is my wife, for sharing the kind of love, patience, and character that has inspired me—to just be me. My family, for exemplifying the traits of integrity, kindness, and generosity . . . some of which has rubbed off on me. And to my friends and colleagues, the ones who cared more about my growth than my comfort and were willing to step in when I stepped out of line. I am forever grateful to all of you.

Introduction

I'm sure you've noticed that life isn't just moving fast today; it's continually accelerating! Keeping pace and trajectory to make sure all areas of our life are healthy, growing, and moving in the right direction is difficult. Our goals are under constant attack with change, competition, busyness, and distraction. And yet, the total combined effect of all this external noise is fractional compared to what takes place between our own two ears. Our perspectives determine how we feel, think, act, and perform.

That's why I first created ShiftPoints: (1) to share simple perspectives that bring a clarity and understanding to how we process the day-to-day, and (2) to help you move from Point A—wherever that is—to Point B in just about every category of life. Ironically, it's the subtle shifts in how we think that can turn limitations into opportunities, walls that stop us into piles of debris, fears that rock our world into confidence that rules it, and the stresses of life into joys of the heart. ShiftPoints will interrupt the thoughts that don't serve you and introduce new ways of thinking to help you improve your life. That's the point of ShiftPoints . . . to *shift*!

I originally started writing ShiftPoints as an email communication for Breviti, my branding agency. And since I began, I've received thousands of comments about how these ideas have been instrumental in improving people's thought life and changing their lives. My hope is that they will impact yours in an immediate and powerful way. I believe they will.

The Anatomy of a ShiftPoint

ShiftPoints are brief, digestible reflections that bring reality and direction to our communication, relationships, integrity, vision, and more. In contrast to reading a whole book to get the point, each ShiftPoint is written strategically with topics distilled down to an applicable principle that can be acted on immediately. The end of each ShiftPoint is designed to be a new beginning, by taking what you read on the pages of this book and writing it into the story of your life—with new words, new actions, and a fresh way of experiencing life, no matter what condition your life is in.

Reading *Shift Your Thinking* Is a Pace, Not a Race

To read *Shift Your Thinking* from cover to cover in one sitting would cause severe cerebral overload. It's not meant to be read that way. Rather, there are a couple of different ways to approach this book more effectively. You could:

A. Read one ShiftPoint a day and work on it.
B. Read a few, then pick one to work on.
C. Read until one moves you to act, based on what is relevant, compelling, and real for you.

Regardless of method, the goal is to meditate on what you read, see how it resonates with your life, and act with intentionality. With brevity in mind, read at whatever pace works for you . . . it's your call, it's your life. But here's what I'll promise you: Once you read the first two dozen entries in this book and begin applying what you read, you will see results in short order.

P.S. How You Can Make a Difference with ShiftPoints

During the course of reading this book, you may discover points that you believe will help someone you know—friends, family, co-workers, etc. Pass that point along—this book is about making a difference! Before you do, though, read the final ShiftPoint on page 215 for best results.

Shift now, shift well, and shift *forward*!

—Dean

People have many brands they can choose from. You are one of them!

If you were a brand, would you buy yourself or keep shopping?

You may not give it much thought, but you are a "brand" to everyone who knows you. Your personal brand is always speaking, and like all brands, it is subject to constant scrutiny and potential breakdown. Comprising your integrity, way of being, and, of course, your track record in day-to-day life, the way your personal brand resonates with others *will* profoundly impact your relationships, career opportunities, and life momentum. At the same time, your brand can stop you in your tracks if you're not clear about what you stand for and how you will make yourself relevant and beneficial to those around you. Keeping commitments, showing up on time, excellence in work ethic, response times, how you handle the details, and the overall value you create for others are a few of the many ways your brand is measured. And in today's world of constant evaluation, keeping your personal brand intact is vital to sustain your influence, position, and ability to move into new situations with a positive presence and credibility. With as little as a single experience, or a quick search online, your brand *is*, or will soon be, in full view for the world to see. Will viewers be attracted or repelled? Will they buy in or move on? It all depends on the "brand of you" they experience, online or off. Maintaining your personal brand standards and reputation does require work, but the alternative is sometimes a tainted personal brand that is beyond repair. An occasional close look in the mirror, plus honest feedback from others, will help you uncover ways to make your brand more compelling for all concerned.

Make sure your brand aligns with who you are committed to being today!

- *How is my brand affecting others personally, professionally, and socially?*
- *Are there traits or behaviors I need to build into or remove from my personal brand to have better results in life?*

ASAP isn't a commitment—it's confusion.

Ever made a request for something to be done only to hear, "I'll get it done ASAP," or "I'll get back to you ASAP"? Typically we leave these conversations with nothing but uncertainty and confusion about what is real and when things will happen. Truth be told, ASAP is a phrase that doesn't come from anyone who is serious about getting things done. It is a strategy for postponement of work, poor performance, or breaking commitments, and is a chief cause of breakdowns in teams who count on each other to get things completed in a timely manner. ASAP is the vernacular for the semi-committed. It's for those who seem more comfortable living with unspecified promises than they are about giving the gift of clear communication. The phrase ASAP has no specifics or timelines attached to it and shows a lack of concern for others' commitments and responsibilities. It's a form of ambiguity that, in the end, will require more work than being clear in the first place . . . much more work . . . and anxiety . . . and relational conflicts, and, and, and. How much more effective could we be if every commitment and conversation were specific?

People appreciate it when we tell them what's real. They are able to stay accountable, share details of the commitment with others, and track progress along the way. Case in point: If you were in need of a critical medicine for a deadly infection, would you rather hear, "I'll get it to you ASAP," or "You'll have it today by 2:00 p.m."? The remedy for life productivity and stress reduction rests largely on what we can count on, and counting on ASAP just isn't possible.

Say good-bye to ASAP, ASAP. Whoops!

- *In what areas of life do I avoid responsibility by being vague?*
- *What price do I and others pay for my unclear or incomplete commitments?*

Many opportunities for learning have been missed because we insisted on talking and talking and talking.

If we're really honest, there are few things in life more gratifying than when we say something cool, smart, or relevant—something that others get value from and that makes us look good for a fleeting moment. But if the same conversational energy and focus were used to be inquisitive and to learn from those around us, the "moment of looking good" would pale in comparison to the learning value we would derive from each conversation. Don't get me wrong; talking intelligently is a valuable asset. But talking too much, and listening too little, can have those around us looking for the exit sign, whether our words are intelligent or not. What's worse is we miss so much when we get in the mode of a one-way broadcast and disregard the value of intentional listening and the art of inquiry.

Admittedly, there are times when I'm talking that I get caught up in trying to convince others (and myself) that I am smart. In fact, during some conversations, I'll usually keep talking until I'm semi-sure what I said is deemed as intelligent. That can take awhile, and the victim on the other end of my monologue frankly doesn't deserve to be caught up in my insecure need to be viewed as something special. Then there are times when I focus intently on listening, and although it's not as fun as talking, I'm always *assured* to be more intelligent than I ever am when talking. Another benefit is that the other person will leave the conversation feeling valued and will think I am smart for listening. The truth is, everything I ever wanted to know or needed to know *could* have been learned by simply listening.

Listen more and talk less today. See what you learn;
see how others respond.

- *When and where do I feel the need to do more talking than listening?*
- *How effective am I at drawing out what is fascinating about people?*

When you begin to think less about what people think of you, that's when you'll be able to really think!

Does your worry over what others think of you hinder your ability to think clearly and peacefully?

If we measured how much of our thought life is caught up in what others think of us, we'd come up with a percentage. There's always a level of effort we put into climbing on the stage of life and performing to gain the approval of others. Sometimes it's a small amount; other times it consumes us and causes unnecessary relational strain. It's human nature to want to be valued. But when others' approval becomes a source of anxiety, insecurity, and self-focus—taking away precious mental energy—it's time to rethink the value of that attention. So rather than refining our performances in life and polishing the plastic, our time would be better spent refining the process of being fully ourselves, whatever that looks like.

Take the risk, and just be. Climb off the mental jungle gym of circumstantial acting and exercise the courage to just let *you* flow through. Although you may hit some "you" snags, which you will, you'll be refining and polishing truth, not a lie, performance, or façade. You'll feel like you've lost a ton of emotional baggage. Your relationships will be more rewarding, and you'll discover a level of peace you may have thought was gone forever.

I once pictured myself lying in my grave, asking, "Was all the fear and distraction I experienced being wrapped in others' perception of me worth it, and did it add value to my life? Did all the façades I presented impress anyone or add value to anything?" The answer was no, and I realized hindsight can be 20/20, even if imagined.

Forget about what people think of you. Be fully yourself today, and see how people respond.

- *How much time do I spend making an impression vs. making a difference?*
- *Will I take a week or so to test what it would be like to be completely me?*

What if the career move you were fantasizing about was just your current career, but with a more rigorous level of commitment?

The old saying that the grass is greener on the other side is a nice line, but it fails to define what is over on the other side once we get there. Those greener pastures may not be as green as we thought, especially when we no longer have the tools of perspective or experience we had on the previous side. So we end up in a new thing with old baggage and a whole host of new challenges we weren't expecting, most of which are exactly like the ones we left on the original side.

To be blunt, the "other side," as we call it, is often a mirage, an illusion that something new will mean something great and that change will magically remove obstacles and will somehow develop new character traits in us. It rarely does. Let's face it—tough times are notorious for tempting us with the distraction of "I think I need to move to the next thing in life." But if we measured the amount of time we spent fantasizing about "the next thing," we'd discover the actual reason why our "current situation" is in the shape it's in. Diversion is a liability to the present. If we took the time that we wasted on daydreaming and applied that time and focus to what is now, the grass on this side would get watered immediately and would become greener before we know it. Don't get me wrong; contemplating the future isn't all bad. But when daydreaming distracts you from being responsible with the present, not only will you lose sight of what's possible, your current dream will likely become the nightmare it was never meant to be.

Maximize present circumstances and see what is possible today.

- *Am I giving my present circumstances the commitment they deserve?*
- *Is daydreaming about change causing my current realities to suffer?*

Don't let television take all the vision from your life.

Is watching less TV a "remote" possibility?

Seventy-five years ago a little black box entered the home. For a few seasons families surrounded it together, but before long families could afford another one, two, or five. Family members split into their own rooms, each with their own black box, and thus, a very insidious division of the family began. Family goals and activities got shelved for the sake of *The Honeymooners* or some other chewing gum for the brain. Tragic! If ever a device has robbed more life, vision, and potential from people and families, it would be the television (aka take-a-vision). Lost in news, sitcoms, and reality shows are hobbies, goals, and relational growth. Things or people we've wanted to invest in just have to wait because *The Voice* is on in ten. Two hours and a thousand calories later, our life-vision is a bit more blurred while TV puts us further into a fog. With all the options to watch and the ability to buy a TV for the price of a pair of sneakers, it's a pandemic issue, and TV is doing everything it can to keep you glued to the box. Its finances depend on it, and "Big Television," by nature of its increasingly carnal content, has no interest in your family or your goals in life. Its interest is in ratings, pure and simple. Are they evil? Of course not. They can't take away our choice. But do consider that by the time a person hits age sixty-five, they'll have spent about eight years watching TV . . . or one-eighth of their life.

Do the math: New careers have been learned in a year, billion-dollar businesses built in three years, books written in six months, relationships reinvigorated in one month, and the list goes on. TV is an addiction that will steal your potential. It will sideline you from the richness of life, love, relationships, and passions as surely as the remote has become a sixth appendage.

- *Which of my passions and goals are sidelined because TV is center stage?*
- *Are there TV programs that can actually enrich my life and my goals?*

Subtle changes in the words we use can make a serious difference in the results.

Words come out of our mouths at a pretty rapid pace at times, and the faster they come out, the less productive or more damaging they can be. Most of us are in the habit of letting our mouths run at the pace of our *emotions* instead of our *thoughts*. Yet a little thought goes a long way in taming the delivery of our words. To be candid, we can say almost anything to anyone as long as it is said in such a way that it can be heard.

For example, when my wife and I were trying to cut expenses for a few seasons, I was scrutinizing the credit card bills and noticed (at least to me) an astonishing number of trips to the salon, the spa, and the beauty shop. The total monthly dollar amount was substantial. Now, I love my wife, and I didn't want her to think I was blaming her, as I have my own expense issues. I wanted to approach her with a caring heart and be effective at the same time. So when we sat down, I said the following: "Honey, you know we're on this expense-reduction kick, and I was looking through your monthly expenses, and I finally figured out how it is I have the hottest wife on the planet." She gave me a sheepish grin, and we both laughed, made some adjustments, and moved on. It could have been catastrophic, but instead it was fun simply by adding a little forethought and creativity to the mix.

Note these subtleties in communication: "Make me an offer on that" vs. "Make me a *fair* offer on that." "You're a loser" vs. "You're losing in life." "Get some milk on the way home" vs. "Honey, could you do me a favor and pick up some milk?" "You're a flake" vs. "You're making it hard for me to do business with you." No matter what the circumstance, there's always a way to say it that will work better than emoting.

Keep an eye, and a heart, on what you say today.

- *Is my mouth controlled by my emotions or by my character?*
- *Will I challenge myself to use more wisdom with my words?*

Those who value people over profits will profit from those people.

Are people primarily a means to satisfy yourself, or are you about bringing value to people?

In the world of business, the question "Will I get further if I take from people or give to them?" bounces back and forth between the lines of selfishness and selflessness. Frankly, progress in the corporate world can be made both ways, but true peace and prosperity in life are rarely found in a taking stance vs. a giving stance. In the long run, profitable, durable relationships are ones where giving is more present than taking. Relationships are the heartbeat of business. They grow the company, profit the bottom line, and assure the brand equity of both the business and the individual. A single relational breakdown can make or break a career or a business.

I must admit that for many years of my business life, people were just a means to my end, nothing more. People were what they could give me, and my relationships were empty, my life had no balance, and I was successful and yet miserable in every moment. Yes, I had assets, but I also had loneliness in volumes that made everything I owned nothing more than a means to escape the relational dysfunction I was living in and the pain that went along with it. So rather than my assets being a blessing, they were merely a numbing agent for my pain. Enough of that. When I realized that people were more important than my vision and goals, and that I could make a difference in their vision and goals, true success set in. Not just in the form of cash, but in peace, joy, relationships, and *real* future potential.

Value people over your agenda today.

- *How do I use people in my life, and how does that impact my relationships?*
- *What would valuing people over profits look like for me?*

Profanity is nothing more than a momentary lapse in creativity.

I've always wondered who used the first curse word and how profanity evolved. Think about it. It had to start off with a single word in a single circumstance. For some reason it caught on, and we now have enough words and phrases to create a profanity dictionary.

We may never know the origin of the thousands of curse words and phrases, but they are here, and the way I see it, profanity *does* have many uses. Sometimes we use it to relieve stress or make us feel good. Mostly it's used to emphasize points, to embed more intensity or impact into our communication. We also use profanity in conversation as a tool—albeit a dull one.

The tragic part of profanity is that it generally shows up in the most emotional, opportune parts of a conversation, a time where life or death can be brought forth in the power of words. It's in these moments where we're faced with a legitimate growth opportunity:

to default to profanity or choose to innovate creative or new content that has equal or greater value and impact than a few expletives. We think profanity opens up conversation, but really it closes minds, shuts down possibility, bears poor witness, and in a subversive manner, makes us feel smaller and less intelligent when we use it. It puts our power in expletives rather than in more powerful, poignant statements.

What could happen if we struggled to exercise our minds rather than indulge in a bit of verbal lack? Consider verbal self-control a discipline for character, creativity, and better communication. Consider it an option that all will appreciate if we replace profanity with something more rewarding than a split second of feel-good indignity.

**Replace any profanity with
conversational creativity today.**

- *Can I go a day, a week, a month without using profanity?*
- *Could I improve my self-control, my vocabulary, and my social
  standing if I paid more attention to my words?*

Do clever quotes have power?
In "deed" they do.

So many quotes, so little action, so many sayings, so little traction! Most of us are intrigued with quotes. We enjoy them because someone cared enough to reduce the word count, so they're a quick study and only take a few seconds. And usually someone cared enough to write them in a way that is clever, humorous, or in-your-face . . . in a good way. The combination of brevity and impact also makes quotes retainable. But quotes, sayings, even ShiftPoints are meaningless unless they engage the reader and move them to action. In reading any quote, the value isn't in the feeling you get, the cleverness of the words, or who said it, although that adds to the emotional bling factor. The real value of a quote that touches you is spending a few additional moments to see how it can apply to your life and to those in it, and to see how the creative thoughts will manifest out of your thoughts into real life. The goal of any quote strong enough to take up some memory space in our minds is to make it become real and deliver it into the world so it can touch the lives of those around us. There's always something or someone who will benefit if you take the principle that moved *you* and put it in play so it moves others. In fact, anyone who ever wrote a quote (dead or alive) wished or wishes only one thing—that the words that were so carefully written would enter the heart and mind of the reader and move them to adjust, impact, transform, grow, lead, change, or improve. So remember, a quote in *heed* is a quote in *deed*. Yeah, you can quote me on that.

Think of your favorite quote and breathe life into it today.

• *Am I living out my favorite quotes, or are they collecting dust in my head?*
• *What one quote will I live out in the next thirty days?*

Gratefulness = Great Fullness!

To be grateful about what we have is to lose focus on what we have not.

We live in a society where contentment and gratefulness seem like the rarest of antiquities. The never-ending quest for better and more has us blowing through days in a frenetic chase for what is already in front of us, only we're too wrapped up in what we don't have to value what we do.

Case in point: Sitting on the couch, my wife chimed in, "Have you considered lately how much we have to be grateful for?" Fact is, I'd been busy with work, was serving on multiple boards, was busy with ministry work, and I hadn't given it too much thought for quite some time. So I took a little break from the chaos (about seven actual minutes of concentrated thought), and I reflected on the blessings we shared; the relationship my wife and I had together; our family, friends, ministry, career, etc. In a few short minutes of taking inventory of what was nothing more than real in my life, I experienced an intense level of contentment I hadn't felt for quite some time, and yet nothing had changed—no winning lottery ticket, no big deal closed, no great vacation to look forward to. In fact, nothing special was happening at all in that moment—nothing but a concentrated dose of clarity of what was already so and what I already had. After only a few minutes of contemplation, it dawned on me that stress, pressure, self-doubt, whining, and every other negative, real or invented, could never coexist in the same space as gratefulness. To be in a state of that awareness pushed everything that depreciated my present circumstances right out into the crapmosphere . . . where it belongs.

Experience the fullness of remaining grateful today.

- *When was the last time I took inventory of the blessings in my life?*
- *What might I be missing now because I am too wrapped up in distractions?*

Adversity is the tuning fork of our lives.

I've been thinking of petitioning to change the spelling of adversity to *add*versity. Frankly, the value of adversity has an amazing way of *add*ing things to our character and our attitude that nothing else can, as long as we are willing to consider the value therein. In every conflict, there are pearls of learning, wisdom, healing, and more, but our instincts must move from "This is bad" to "This is potential," where our quick response focuses on the *solution* and *opportunities* rather than the *problem*.

Believe it or not, one of the better things that ever happened to me was losing 70 percent of my company's revenue in the span of a week. Friday afternoon, 4:00 p.m., *poof*! Nine million in annual revenue—gone, with a huge overhead still yelling, "Feed me." Add to that we were at an interim location, building a 21,000-square-foot facility, needing to downsize by forty people . . . oh, and I almost forgot, my second-biggest client called two weeks later to tell me they had decided to develop an in-house marketing department.

Here's the kicker. I wouldn't trade the experience for anything in the world. It was during the decline that I learned leadership, grace, sensitivity, trust, and patience . . . all because a close friend of mine had said, "Don't let this test *not* turn into a testimony." So I went into work the following Monday looking at the glass half full instead of the bank account almost empty, and was able to turn a potential tragedy into a fulfilling new reality on many levels.

Discover the value in your adversity today!

- *What is my standard reaction when problems surface? Embrace or repel?*
- *What one problem area of my life could use a bit of new thinking?*

If we gossiped about ourselves for a week, we might never gossip again.

Ahhhh, gossip. Sometimes it's just plain fun to rip on someone— that is, until the words actually come out of our mouths and we feel the shame and guilt of the indulgence. The temptation to gossip is only surpassed by the inventory of material there is to work with. Through our social circles and the abundance of media distribution channels, there are endless opportunities to engage in gossip—gossip that breeds nothing but internal conflict and indifference to others. What a poor reflection of our personal brand!

The dictionary definition of gossip is "spreading rumors or opinions of someone's personal affairs, usually without their knowledge or all the facts." But in street terms, gossip takes on a whole new meaning that should motivate us to never speak ill of someone again . . . *ever*. In the practical sense, gossip is (1) speaking about others in terms of hopelessness, pessimism, and indifference simply because of our limiting belief that people can't change; (2) sharing about others without any real discernment of what is going on in their lives; (3) proclaiming others' failures for the sake of edifying our own perceived position or success; (4) arrogantly denying our own brand of screwed-up, by which we entertain a ridiculous sense of self-righteousness; and (5) setting a poor example to others no matter how artful and clandestine we think we are when doing it. When we gossip, it accurately reflects our social status and the condition of our hearts more than we think. It says something about *us* that is much more despicable than anything we could say of another and is toxic waste to social circumstances.

Today, replace gossip with words that bring life, not strife.

- *Am I one to make light of others' troubles?*
- *When gossip reveals itself, do I add fuel to the fire or do I put the fire out?*

We are all born to be brilliant, only to be sabotaged by *average*.

*A*verage is out, just like leg warmers are out. But unlike average, leg warmers might just make a comeback. (Ouch!) Today, average is so far in the backdrop, it hardly gets noticed, and when seen it is generally the victim of ridicule or avoidance. And yet many are still trying to get by with average and are getting further behind in life. I don't know about you, but when I go to a store, I never ask the clerk for an average product or service. When I considered marriage, I never thought, *Boy, if I could just find an average wife.* And when I go to a nice restaurant, I never ask for an average meal. Average has lost its credentials in *all* areas of life.

There was a time when we could get by with average, but in today's world it is never more uninspiring than to strive for *OK*. No matter what your position in life, the quest for average is not a goal—it's a retreat. It lives quietly, passively, teetering on the brink between *hope* and *hopelessness*. It's a tentative posture with nothing to commend it, a numbed-out way of life unfortunately practiced by many. In contrast, the quest for an amazing life, extraordinary love, and exemplary commitments brings with it focused goals and clarified vision. It lives on the edge of *something big* or *something bigger*, and it teeters back and forth between passion and purpose, progress and prosperity. There's something big in all of us, and it is only our quest for average that keeps it sleeping.

Live fully in the brilliance you are today.

- *Am I more interested in surviving than thriving?*
- *What would life be like if my activities were flourishing rather than floundering?*

Never underestimate the transformation that can come from a single "new experience."

One of the reasons I wrote a book on shifting the way we think about things is because the mind is a life-changing tool, capable of empowering us to unfathomable achievements. At the same time, if our thinking is compromised due to a lazy human at the helm of the mind, we can be equally empowered to do nothing, and do *that* extraordinarily well.

Although paradigm shifts are among the most powerful and proactive ways to improve our lives, there are other ways to grow and prosper, and that is simply deciding ourselves into new experiences. New experiences can be even more powerful than paradigm shifts or other personal development methods including books, workshops, and seminars. The good news is that the opportunities for new experiences are endless—like helping the homeless, skydiving, traveling to a foreign land, taking a shooting class, or engaging in a hobby. When we live out a new experience (no matter what it is) we get to live life from the place of that new experience. It's the kind of growth that just happens to you. Typically, any one new experience will tune, build, and develop us into more confident, adventurous people; it will give us a new place to live from, and that will affect change in every area of our life.

Identify a *new* experience and put it on the calendar today.

• *What holds me back from taking steps to new life experiences?*
• *What one experience have I been considering that I can commit to?*

Start your day in a quiet zone,
before your mind-set becomes a riot zone.

Almost every human being would admit they'd like better ideas and clearer perspectives in life, if only they had access to such revelation. Well, *we do*. Such insight is found in our opportunity to leverage the value that resides in peace—peace that can make every day more efficient, effective, and enjoyable if we take the time to slow down and access each day's potential. Unfortunately, the start of every day is something we take lightly, and too many people wake up at full throttle with one foot to the floor and one out the door, anemically prepared for the realities of life, only to do it again the following day. Often we ignore the opportunity to get up a little earlier, create the space to stretch out our minds, and calmly think through the details of our day. Instead, we land smack-dab in the middle of the day, forced to work out life on the fly. Urgency takes charge and throws us into "survive mode," when with a little foundational morning work we could move through the day in "thrive mode."

Real progress comes when you're relaxed rather than stressed. The practice of becoming clear about our way of being, things we will do and not do, and preparing ourselves for all meetings, events, and conversations will improve results—*dramatically*. Thinking through the day and making decisions in advance will mean fewer surprises. It will streamline the time we have into more effective, more efficient, more rewarding days. So take a break after you wake and spend some quiet time to reflect on your day, your relationships, and your responsibilities. Meditate on what you'll be facing, and you'll gain perspectives that will have you starting off on top of your day, rather than letting your day climb on top of you.

**Take some quiet time at the start of every
day to make that day a better day.**

• *Will I carve out some time in the morning to think through my day?*

- *What parts of my day need to be thought out with a more concerted effort?*

Growth in one area of our life while the others suffer is *not* self-development——it's self-centeredness.

There are many areas of life that need our attention: work, spouse, kids, spirituality, health, friendships, ministry, hobbies, social activities, and fun. Each are living, breathing entities that need an infusion of care every day; otherwise they wither and die. Keeping these categories of life balanced is no small task, for within each are many factors and considerations, as well as endless moving parts and emotions. They get out of balance when some are ignored while we give attention to others, and it happens as easily as breathing. Work is usually the culprit of stealing time from the rest, but focusing on *any* one of these areas while the others take a backseat is the beginning of a life out of harmony. It is generally a move toward the kind of selfishness that leads to emptiness. We tend to migrate toward the things we *want* to do rather than the things we *should* be doing, and the result is not a dividend as much as a division.

Admittedly, the decision to make sure all areas grow in sync means that all areas will grow a bit slower. This is a fact and a test of our patience. But when all areas of life are winning, then peace is present, joy is abundant, and true success surrounds you. Life is no longer a race being run on the ups and downs of adrenaline; it's a pace where our commitment to enhancing all areas adds blessing and creates fulfillment that could never be attained through any *one* area of great success. Ever!

Consider the condition of all the categories
of your life today.

- *Which areas of my life are spiking while the others are hurting?*
- *Will I quality-check each of these areas or ignore them until they die off?*

Winning the argument isn't worth losing the intimacy.

Unless you like to argue, and there are those who do, I'm sure you'd agree that life would be better if heated arguments and tantrums could be shifted to cool, calm discussions that eliminate yelling, throwing things, and stomping out of the room. The key is to understand our will and our role in arguments. Our personal will isn't a bad thing. In fact, our will is a driving force for many great things in life and can even be directed *toward* reconciliation and healing in relationships. But when it becomes unbendable or self-righteous, it can become a destroyer of relational progress and perhaps of the relationship itself.

It helps to accept that in just about every conflict, both parties contribute to the problem at different levels at different times. Sometimes our contribution to the problem is low on the percentage scale; other times it reaches near 100 percent. But trust me, there's a percentage of our own nonsense in every argument, whether we see it that way or not.

Regardless, searching for how we may have contributed to or played a role in the breakdown and confessing our part creates the space for conversation to move into trust and humility instead of blame, and it shows a commitment to own up to our stuff. This revelation can take the sting out of arguments and point our will toward relational solidarity rather than living on the edge of conflict at every turn. But conflicts will happen, so while in the thick of them, our will should focus on making a difference, not making the other pay; taking responsibility, not taking advantage; and getting it right while not always needing to be right.

> **Make sure your will is about breaking down walls, not building them higher.**

- *Does my will lean more toward reconciliation or being right?*
- *What would arguments be like if I first confessed my contribution to them?*

If you want to be spontaneous, plan for it!

With life's busyness getting busier by the nanosecond, you'd think the desire or even the need to be spontaneous would be more common. But it's not. The active nature of today's daily lifestyle has most people worn out before they check out, clock out, or schlep out of their jobs. The notion of being spontaneous is taking second fiddle to the fatigue that follows our busy lifestyles. I figure the best-case scenario for being spontaneous is to plan for it: Bring in new things and get them on the calendar so they feel spur-of-the-moment through their newness. It's hard to get off the dime when you can't even get off the couch! In that case, spontaneity needs a bit of planning.

I know some would call this a cop-out, and it might be. But for me, spontaneity has never been one of my strengths, and I naturally gravitate toward planning everything. It's called anal retentiveness, and yes, I'm *planning* on dealing with it. So in keeping with sticking my neck out vs. stuckness, I have devised a predictable model for being spontaneous.

Here's how we do it. During the week, my wife and I take some time and plan one thing we normally wouldn't do for the coming weekend. The result? We get to experience the newness, adventure, and surprise of spontaneity without actually being spontaneous.

The mind doesn't know the difference, but the excitement of life we get to experience makes a difference that we simply can't ignore. And as creatures of habit, that makes life and all that's in it seem more exciting, more adventurous, and yes, more spontaneous.

Develop your plan to try new things today.

- *On a scale of 1–10, how spontaneous am I?*
- *Can I list ten things I normally wouldn't do and schedule them over ten weeks?*

Changing how we think requires that we think for a change!

If we took inventory of how many times our brains convinced us that a circumstance would turn out badly, and it didn't, we'd discover that our minds can truly have a mind of their own, unless of course, we start to mind our minds. Seems every day random thoughts float around our head, demeaning thoughts that don't have much care or concern for our well-being or progress. Why is that? The hard truth is that we maintain a casual posture with these random, unbridled, but very powerful thoughts, and just like all forces, they can build momentum and strength.

Many people are resigned to the belief that this is how life works, and rather than seeing the potential of taking ownership of their thought life, they allow these thoughts to run free and do their dirty work over and over again. Mark Twain put it brilliantly when he said, "I am an old man who has known a great many troubles, most of which never happened." It seems an hourly occurrence that our minds will invent stress, doubts, and fear regarding what *might* happen, simply because we've allowed the habit of letting our mind have its way with us. The quote "As [a man] thinketh in his heart, so is he" is there to let us know that we can be in control of our mind instead of allowing our mind to rule over us. We forget that our mind is capable of reengineering and refocusing every thought we have into a positive paradigm that drives possibility instead of anxiety. But it requires a few minutes of concentration and the discipline to stop and say to these destructive thoughts, "No, not this time. It's time to rethink this thought for a change."

Invest a few moments to rework every negative thought today.

- *What are the repeated thoughts I have that don't serve me well?*
- *What might a little thought time do to minimize or eliminate these thoughts?*

Self-evaluation is an oxymoron with the emphasis on *moron*.

I am doing a good job. I am a great spouse. I am a good friend." Oh really? And what might others have to say about this?

Some people go a lifetime without ever hearing key behavioral feedback from others. The reasons people do not speak up vary: Most don't have the courage to deliver raw truth, or they don't know how to say it, or they're not equipped to provide it. It is rare these days to receive the critical feedback that can help us see our blind spots, so we often resort to self-evaluation as the pollution—I mean, *solution*. Not that introspection is bad, but it goes without saying that our opinions of ourselves can be overrated, just as they can be underrated. The survival instinct we maintain is always going to protect and defend the opinions we have of ourselves. But are these opinions accurate, or are they biased by past circumstances, insecurities, pride, and other factors?

If we want to get the critical evaluation we need to improve in just about every area of our lives, we need to create the space for others to be honest with us and allow them to tell us what is on their minds without being defensive. That is the quickest, most effective way. The more honest the feedback, the more valuable it is. Not that what others say is always right; it is just one person's experience of you, and that is as real for them as it gets. But if two or more deliver the same message, the evaluation carries much more weight. Take it as truth and consider it a blessing that you heard it and can now act on it. Although feedback can hurt for the moment, the most damaging feedback is that which, for some reason, never gets delivered.

Create the space to get some feedback on one area of your life today.

- *Who do I trust to give me feedback in various areas of my life?*
- *Who will be the first one for whom I'll create the space to receive honest feedback?*

People are in awe of those who simply stay in the present.

There are social discomforts that are completely unnecessary and make life awkward, stressful, and unfulfilling. And the winners are—living life in the past, lusting for what is to come, or simply being distracted by things going on in the moment. These are the conversation killers and are the end of what could be a great encounter, or even a great relationship with someone. For example, have you ever conversed with someone who lives in the past? Draining, isn't it? It seems like the conversation is going backward and you feel like you're being pulled down a funnel into nowhere . . . simply exhausting.

Now, how about someone too caught up in their future? Hard to keep up, yes? These conversations feel like you're being dragged behind a horse in the desert with no control or perspective of when it will end.

Now how about someone who makes you feel like you're the only person on the planet when you're in their presence? Rare, yes! Inspiring, absolutely. Being with people like this is rare indeed, but it is among the most rewarding experiences in life. When someone is present with us, it makes us feel at ease and valued. It allows us to be fully ourselves.

Now consider that we have the capacity to give that same gift to others. And we do. It takes great focus, care, and discipline to stay present with people. But the payoff is big. You create rapport, trust, and opportunity. People leave the conversation feeling valued. You leave it feeling honorable, fulfilled, and knowing you did the right thing.

**Be present with others and fight
being distracted today.**

- *Do I drift to the past or the future in conversation, or do I just get distracted?*
- *Do I do any service to the things I'm thinking about when I drift?*

Comparison is no measure of success.

Society at large places great emphasis on comparison. From products to services to brands to people, comparisons are at work and never stop. Comparison is both tireless and tiring, as the comparisons available online and off are endless, overwhelming, and not always very accurate. On the human side, comparison is the trap of contrasting ourselves to others we generally know little or nothing about.

How does this comparison work? To say I am rich because I am not living on the street is comparison. To say I am blessed because I'm not a starving child in Africa is comparison. To say I am attractive because I am not ugly like someone I consider to be ugly is comparison. Real success is never measured by comparison. Comparisons are a trap that will have us in an endless game of emotional ping-pong. Even further, there are just too many comparisons in existence, and we could spend a lifetime posturing ourselves against someone or something with underwhelming results and no real accuracy as to who we really are. The only genuine measure of success in life is whether or not we are living in the full potential of who we are regardless of how limited or great our capacity, looks, ability, etc. Comparison is the measure we rely on when our potential in life is either out of focus or isn't being exercised. True success comes from operating in the fullness of our talents, abilities, and God-given gifts. It's in the stretching, risking, and living in our potential that comparison loses any and all meaning, and that our potential trumps our need to use others as the determining factor of our worth, and that means everything compared to . . . Whoops!

Replace the disease of comparison with the progress found in living out your potential today.

- *Am I caught up in measuring myself by comparison or by my potential?*
- *When was the last time I looked at my potential? Do I even know what it is?*

If you're looking to find yourself, look at what shows up in other people as you engage with them.

When it comes to finding one's self, there seems to be a myriad of philosophies and methods, ranging from somewhat pragmatic to near insane, and most of them involve some kind of "get away from it all" strategies. Well, I have some smelling salts for you: The quest to find one's true self is a whole lot easier and more relevant than a trip to the Dalai Lama. Ironically, the journey of self-discovery is rarely thousands of miles away from anything; it's usually a few feet away—in our homes, on our streets, and at our work. Every conversation and interaction that we have with someone is an opportunity to discover ourselves by what manifests in the other—in the moment and over time. The effects of our words, actions, and commitments will reveal who we are in ways that make the mystical smoke-and-mirrors methods appear empty and self-serving.

The practice of paying attention to what shows up in others as a result of our behavior can facilitate accurate self-discovery in a matter of seconds, not years, and one does not have to go halfway around the globe. For example, when I make someone smile, I get to find myself in their smile. When I make an impact on someone's life, I find myself in their progress and development. When I share truth with someone, I find myself in the truth that they share back. On the flip side, when I make someone angry, I get to see myself show up in their frustration. When I hurt or confuse someone, I get to see myself revealed in their pain . . . and "sow" on, and "sow" forth. It is a simple sowing and reaping principle, meaning others are the measure of how we show up, and those results matter, not philosophies and hypotheticals.

**Evaluate how you are showing up in others'
lives today, and discover your real self.**

- *Am I willing to look at my interactions with others as the gauge of who I am?*
- *If I evaluated how I impact others' lives, what then would I think of myself?*

The quickest path forward can be found in being straightforward.

Ever since political correctness came along, the way in which we deliver our truth is whitewashed with obscurity, and the values by which we live life are rarely being shared with any real level of conviction. It's all becoming blasé. Political correctness—the practice of self-protection, cover-up, and masking our truth into statements of nothing—is making life beige, blurry, and bleak. Not to say that basic social graces are out of vogue, but to converse with someone who has packaged their speech with intense sanitation is like eating a six-course dinner absent of taste. Pass the salt *please*. Ahhhh, forget it. *Check* please!

As a nation, we've become conversationally contrived, believing that if we step over the line with some conversational smelling salts, there's no turning back. Quite the contrary. It's all but a fact that people would rather be with those who simply share their truth at risk of being wrong or looking foolish over those who design their conversations around looking good, protecting self, appearing intelligent, and offending no one. It's the "what you see is what you get" breath of fresh air that brings life to people and tunes society to deal in directness, not deception. Of course, a little tact and contemplation go a long way in making sure the fullness of our truth is heard. Mark my words, as each year of this complex new world passes, the popularity of political correctness is going to dip below dirt, and the thirst and implicit need for "give it to me straight" is going to spike through the atmospheric shield. The courage to put your full truth on the table will be among the most valued assets on the planet. In fact, it already is.

Have the courage to say what you mean today.

• *Do I package my comments so neatly that nothing actually gets said?*

- *Will I speak the fullness of my truth, knowing that truth can set me free?*

We fear what we're unwilling to manage.

You'll read about fear in this book more than once because it is the most paralyzing emotion that exists. It is proven to keep us from our hopes, dreams, and vision in every area of life, and if that isn't bad enough, its subversive nature can cause disease, anxiety, depression, and suicide. So forgive the redundancy, which I believe is warranted; fear is a human condition that may adjust, but it never goes away completely. Like money managers who manage your money, you've been inherently hired to manage your fear. So what's the status of your job performance in the fear management sector? Are you more on the promotion side, getting fired, or just stuck? You'd have to look at each area of your life to assess how you are dealing with fears, putting them in a place where you largely run *them* and don't allow them to run *you*. Finances, relationships, career, social life, whatever—if we don't have a commitment to managing the fear that shows up in these areas of our life, it's only a matter of time before fear seeps in to paralyze progress. With so many areas of life demanding attention, it's wise to have a system to maintain all of them—in order to keep fear under management. Discovering which areas need attention and then blocking out time to confront the issues, as well as seeking perspective from others, will help you govern over them with excellence, confidence, and reduced anxiety. More on this later.

Start managing the fear that's not being managed today.

- *Where does fear show up on a consistent basis?*

• *Will I invest time to deal with recurring fears or tolerate a lifetime of them?*

Sometimes we don't even recognize when we are complaining.

I'm so sick of people complaining! How's that for hypocrisy?

Why do we complain? The answers are pretty basic, but pretty in-your-face. First, we complain because we believe our unique style of complaining is creative or artistic enough to be appreciated. Yes, for some people complaining is an art-form, but actually it's more of a heart-storm—a condition of a burdened heart that needs to sound off in the form of spewing hopelessness and negativity into a world that could use a little less.

We also complain because of an insecure need to be validated or to be right, which requires others to see our point of view. So complaining becomes a project to convert others to our way of thinking. It's an endless battle, and so there's endless complaining.

Then there's the reality that we complain because we don't have the courage to go beyond the complaint and confront the issue or the person(s) in a way that would be responsible and productive.

But most critically, we complain because we see no greater potential coming from our mouths than the act of complaining itself. While in the heat of a gripe, we can't think of anything productive to say, so our verbal vomit winds up hitting whoever is in its path. Although it may sound like I have a gripe with complaining, I actually condone it . . . in the right setting, with the right people, and with a clear purpose.

I'm convinced complaining can be healthy and appropriate if the complaint we share with others is for the purpose of getting honest and forthright counsel on how to deal with this issue we're complaining about, or they've agreed to allow us to vent. It's also important to share these things in the right setting, where no one is in earshot of the complaint. Ahhhh, complaining—sport for some, false necessity for others. So let's rest on a derivation of an old adage: We have nothing to complain about but complaints themselves.

Show a little complaint restraint today.

- *Is my inclination when annoyed to complain or to offer intelligent perspective?*
- *What constant complaints do I have that I could remove from my life?*

If you want to improve your relationships, discover, deliver, and repeat!

For those who are wise, life is one big, ongoing discovery process—the more the discovery, the more the progress. I call it the velocity of curiosity. It is a process that should never end, only begin. We should be grounded both in its value if we do it and the negative results of moving through life and relationships without the habit of discovery in play. The habit of non-discovery will pin us into a continual state of aloofness, and our value to others will be minimal and inconsistent.

In addition to having my own stories, I've listened to hundreds of tales of personal and business relationships that have gone flat, gone bad, or are just gone, period. After every story, I'm always inclined to ask the same questions. The first is: "Well, what was important to them?" What I get back are blank stares, confusion, and statements like, "Who cares about them? What about me?" Once I clarify "what about me" might be the problem, I'll inquire, "When was the last time you asked what was important to them?"

Answers range from months to decades. After we determine this would be a good place to start, I'll request they begin discovering what's important, then deliver on what they discover, and we'll meet in a week to see how it's going. Other questions I request they ask the other are, "What's missing from our relationship? What would you like me to stop doing, start doing, and continue doing?"

Improving relationships is a simple process of discovering needs, delivering value, measuring results, and repeating the process with sincerity and consistency.

Discover someone's want or need today and deliver on it.

- *Is my posture in tune with the other's needs or am I too focused on my own?*
- *Who haven't I checked in with lately to discover what is important to them?*

Do you have integrity or selective virtue?

Before anyone can claim they have integrity, it helps to truly understand the meaning of the word. Some think it means *doing* things, like keeping your promises, performing your job well, or staying loyal to your friends. Others think integrity has to do with *not doing* things, like lying, showing up late, or treating people unfairly. All are true. But to understand integrity, let alone claim you have it, the meaning must be specific. Generalities are the enemy of integrity, and specificity is what fuels it and drives it.

Integrity's root meaning comes from the word *integrate*— meaning all things in our life working together toward a common belief system with excellence and consistency. Our belief system, whatever that may be, is the foundation of our integrity. By way of example, mine is the Bible and the principles therein. How I live out biblical principles in all things—including work, family, friendships, social interactions, tasks, duties, and responsibilities—determines whether or not I have integrated my belief system in all these areas, not just the ones that are convenient. Integrity is a high bar, and where most people will claim they have it, if they take a close look, they'll discover they have selective virtue where certain areas of life are adhering to the belief system and others are not. This means we are out of integrity and cannot claim we have it.

No one has complete integrity. It's something you can only practice across the board of your life but can never claim to own. We can and should try to evaluate our own lives and give ourselves a score or a grade for each area. For example, in my career I could be earning an A, but in my family life I might have to give myself a C. Our own evaluations are important, but keep in mind that the real score of how we are doing in the area of integrity comes from others, not ourselves.

Hold integrity as the high bar that it should be today.

- *Can I claim to have integrity or just selective virtue?*
- *What areas of my life are operating at a low grade of integrity?*

If you look at the patterns of your life, do they resemble plaid or pinstripes?

The singular path to chaos is found in going multiple ways at once. Patterns—we've seen beautiful ones that minister to our emotions, and we've seen ones that have us laughing, saying, "What were they thinking?" The patterns of our life and how we live them out are no different. Plaid equals chaos, moving in too many directions at once, with no clear direction except for no direction, resembling a busy four-way traffic signal that's stopped working during rush hour. Pinstripes, by way of contrast, mean alignment, things moving forward in uniformity, no zigzagging, minimal confusion, and the path of least resistance and most progress. Any way you look at it, the patterns of our behavior are the crux of our growth. They have a profound impact on how we feel and experience life, and they impact how much we move forward or not. When we live in "plaid," where busyness becomes confused with productivity, the negative effects on life are substantial.

It's a given that life is meant to be lived, but more importantly, life is meant to be designed. It's the difference between the circumstances of life defining you, and you shaping you and what you'll achieve—by choice and by design. The problem is that we move through days at such a frenetic pace that the creative sketch pad of life sits dusty and blank, untapped for the amazing gifts it has waiting. I believe if we spent as much time each year planning our life as we do our vacations, we'd begin to see that life doesn't have to be a never-ending set of random circumstances crisscrossing to no end. It can be a directed, focused, and rewarding set of events that maximize who we are and what we will achieve.

Put the plaid behaviors away.
Get aligned to a clear vision today!

- *Does my life resemble plaid? If so, how can I switch to pinstripes?*
- *What price do I and others have to pay for my plaid lifestyle?*

Delegation is the art of moving people from "have to" to "want to."

Effective delegation is progress multiplied. Without effective delegation, a leader's ability to get things done is diminished, their capacity to make progress that of a single human. Without the ability to expand innovation through others, we'd likely be riding in horse-drawn carriages today if they were still around . . . the carriages, that is.

Delegation is often misunderstood. People in positions of authority rarely spend time analyzing the effectiveness or heart of their delegation, let alone the three kinds of motivation it creates—reluctant, mute, or inspired. Based on a couple of decades as a business consultant, I'd say that most delegation is missing the "inspiration component," adding just another task to someone's already long to-do list. On top of that, most delegations are set up to lose because we're so caught up in urgency, we don't deliver the little extras needed to set the other person up to win. The result? People to whom we delegate walk away confused, even angry. The little extras include choosing the person who would lean *into* the task, not *away* from it; sharing the specifics of the desired outcome; conveying the importance of the task, and in some cases, explaining why you chose them. Lastly, the heartbeat of delegation is to simply, or extravagantly, acknowledge a job well done so the next time you ask, you'll have some fuel in your delegation tank, a better chance at timely follow-through, and more likely, a job done with total excellence.

Reduce your own perspiration by adding a little inspiration to your delegation today!

- *Will I take the time to delegate well or deal with constant task breakdown?*
- *What things need to be delegated and how will I go about it?*

If you want to keep *all* of your commitments, create an infallible reminder system.

One of the common frustrations we experience is someone making a promise and not keeping it. It causes stress, slows momentum, and brings an uncertainty to situations that just shouldn't be there. From big commitments to small, it seems the size of commitment doesn't matter much; and in some cases, not delivering on the small things is bigger than the occasional broken promise of a big thing. It's Commitment 101 to eliminate forgetfulness as an excuse by setting up a way to remind ourselves. That's easy. But the big culprit of broken commitments has little to do with any systems, formulas, or forgetfulness; it's about caring enough for others to keep your word . . . every time.

Case in point: I once told a woman that she didn't keep her commitments because she was invested more in her convenience than she was in people. She said, "Well, I care, but I simply forget." I replied, "Then you don't care enough to have a system so you don't forget." She conceded. With today's frenetic life pace, it's excusable to forget a thing or two. It's not excusable if it happens repeatedly and you ignore the opportunity to develop a reliable reminder system. Some people like to write; others go digital. Regardless of method, your integrity and your reputation count on you keeping your commitments, even the small ones that can slip through the cracks. Not only does keeping your commitments reflect well on those around you, it is one of the most valuable assets you can build into yourself. Period!

Set up a dependable system to keep track of the commitments you make today.

- *What percentage of commitments do I keep? Do I even keep track?*
- *How much do I really care to keep all my commitments?*

Standing out isn't always outstanding.

There's an old adage that indicates no matter how much we try to impress people, our impressions don't matter that much in the long run, especially if they are a "front" or "manipulation" to get something we want in the moment. Time will weed that out. It also implies that no matter how important we *think* we are to other people, we really *aren't* that important. Callous sounding, yes. But if we had a dollar for every time we thought someone was thinking bad or good about us and they weren't, we'd gain a few thousand bucks . . . a year!

Albeit we are important to others, we are just not as important as we make ourselves out to be. So the basic idea of trying to impress people with our carefully planned schemes doesn't carry much weight. And most people are so inept at trying to impress us that all they do is shut down possibilities rather than open doors. For example, ever meet people who feel the need to name-drop from word one and aren't satisfied unless they know that you know how successful or connected they are? I call these "résumé" conversations, and they are stressful and exhausting. We generally derive value from them only when they end.

But then there are those who are content letting the conversation unfold naturally; they stay present with you, and there are no rough edges or hidden motives. They are pleased to get to know you, and the only agenda they have is to have a non-agenda-based conversation that creates mutual value, trust, and respect. These are among the rarest, most impressive people in the world; the ones you'd like to get to know, do business with, invite to your party, and spend quality time with. Now that's an impression.

Practice the discipline of making an impression without impressing today.

- *Do I feel any pressure to impress others when I'm in conversations?*
- *Could I be fully content being exactly who I am?*

Start small, phase in quick wins, build for scalability, and measure as you grow.

When it comes to launching projects, most start out with a bit of over-optimism, planning to eat the elephant in one bite. This kind of planning may work for the rare few, but typically it is not only unrealistic, but also set up to fail. Generally we know this, but even so, we can be easily swayed by unbridled enthusiasm and ignorant passion, whether our own or from others. Not everyone is going to feel comfortable with going "foot to the floor" off the starting line, nor do many have the capacity or all the facts to move that fast.

Case in point: Whenever clients of my branding agency would be tentative about buying off on an entire proposal, we didn't throw a tantrum because they weren't aligned with our enthusiasm or tell them that this was the only way to get things done. We were wise enough to know that we didn't know all the details of their company and its culture. So even though we would reason with them about the value of a comprehensive approach, if it required that we start small, then so be it. For us it was winning the battle, not the war (at the moment) for both the client and ourselves. We were able to secure many long-term relationships this way. The upside is that it gave everyone more time to plan and score some quick victories. And in most cases, it would end up as a full implementation anyway. However, if we pushed too hard for our agenda, we would never have had the chance for a relationship.

The good news is that the model of starting small, getting quick wins, scaling, and measuring is one that works consistently and predictably. And it builds trust, rapport, and results for lasting growth and progress in all areas of life, not just business.

Kick a project into gear by starting small and gaining some quick wins today.

- *What one goal have I shelved because it seemed too big to accomplish?*
- *What would some quick wins look like for a goal that I have?*

If people matter to you, you'll remember their names.

Think about how you feel when someone you just met remembers your name.

I often hear people say, "I'm horrible at names." I reply, "Consider that you're as good as you choose to be, and depending on what is at stake, you are quite good." I go on to ask, "If there were ten million dollars on the line and all you had to do is remember someone's name, would you succeed?" The answer is always, "Yes!" They say, "I'd repeat it, write it down, tattoo it on my arm; whatever it took, I would remember their name." The truth is that somewhere between "it doesn't matter very much" and "ten million dollars," our priority, ability, and capacity to remember are revealed. This simply means we're capable of remembering names but consider it so unimportant that we choose not to improve the practice.

We have great potential to be socially outstanding on a number of fronts but tend to exercise our skill level based on whom we're with at the moment. We tune in or check out depending on what we believe the payoff to be, and therefore develop no consistency or habit of remembering names. The result is that we remain relationally anemic and miss great potential in establishing rapport with others. The value in remembering people's names is one of the highest social rewards that exists. It is the quickest way possible to let someone you just met know that you care about them and translates to instant trust. The results are nothing short of amazing. Remember that!

Google "Remembering people's names"
and learn about it today.

- *Am I resigned to the lie that I am no good at remembering people's names?*
- *Will I practice this discipline starting today?*

N(ego)tiation.

Most things are pretty much what you negotiate them to be, so it pays to negotiate well.

It's no accident that the word *ego* resides in the word *negotiation*. Nor is it any coincidence that ego and greed are close companions. But negotiations of the ego and greed breed are no picnic. Any transaction that is driven by ego and the desire to win is a relational train wreck waiting to happen, and the collateral damage is always more than what is seen in the transaction. Truth be told, more negotiations have stopped midstream or have blown apart toward the end because someone was bent on squeezing every ounce from the transaction. Even *if* ego-driven deals go through, they often cause an aftermath that precludes future opportunities due to relational division and bitterness. In short, the completion of ego-driven negotiations usually happens once, if it happens at all.

Becoming a master of negotiation isn't rocket science. For starters, think not of yourself but of the other side. Consider what they are looking for, what they don't want, what they might fear, their short- and long-term goals, when they want the negotiation completed, etc. Then with that understanding, begin the process of answering those same questions for yourself. The merger of those realities and the depth of determining the win for both parties will clarify your options and purify what you're asking for. Only then will the presence you bring to the negotiating table be received with trust and acceptance instead of guardedness and skepticism. Whether negotiating your way out of a traffic ticket, getting a date for Friday night, persuading a friend to help you move, or closing a big business deal, negotiation is a constant, and identifying win-wins in advance will always advance more win-wins.

**In negotiations, consider the other first
so the relationship will last.**

• Do I lean toward win-lose in negotiations?
• What do the relationships from past negotiations look like today?

The mark of a great conversationalist is found in more question marks.

How well we communicate with others is the single most important factor to our progress in every area of life. Conversations are the precedence of all things, the engine of life and relationships. However, much of our communication resembles that of a radio where the tuning is from slightly off to full-blown static, mainly because we are talking nervously rather than inquiring diligently and responding appropriately. It's all but a fact that everyone would like to be a better, more strategic communicator—to be able to say things to others that resonate, move things forward, improve relationships, make life easier and more enjoyable. The right words, tone, and manner can do that.

But becoming a master of conversation has little to do with making brilliant statements every time we engage with others. Most of us aren't that smart or that quick, nor do we have enough life experience or skill to be able to speak our way into favor in all circumstances. What makes a conversationalist brilliant is asking great questions . . . a learned skill. Questions are safe, they create insight, and they uncomplicate and improve conversations . . . instantly. It's also amazing how much more interesting people find you when you ask meaningful questions. There are always gifts to be found in great questions.

Talk less, learn more, and ask great questions today.

• Am I more in the habit of making statements or asking questions?
• Do I have a good list of basic social questions to ask people?

Our confidence in meetings
will always be in direct proportion to our preparation.

Life is a series of meetings. From casual to serious, they are the means by which we get things done, or don't. We've all been in meetings where we've been impressed and in others we could have done without (or would even have run from if possible). And yet the combined effectiveness of people and process in a well-tuned meeting has amazing potential if someone comes to the table prepared and is willing to put forth effort, respect the time of all involved, and run a strong meeting.

The outcome of every gathering you lead and its impact on your personal brand hinges on preparation . . . relevant preparation. And not just preparation of the facts, figures, background, materials, and such. Those are important, of course. They are the basics and should be exemplary and consistent. But more to the point, getting clear about who you are—your posture, way of being, and presence—in a meeting is more significant than what you present or say. In truth, your way of being will be the driver and controller of everything that happens in the meeting, good or bad.

And for those who don't consider themselves the best orators, being resolute about what you're committed to causing in the room is more important than how polished you are. And how much you *care* for others in the room will overpower how good your presentation looks.

Lastly, how clear you are about specific steps after the meeting is equally important to the steps you took walking in. Your preparation needs to cover all the bases. Then you'll be armed with the confidence you need to make sure every meeting you lead is a home run, or at least a triple.

Prepare . . . for a better meeting today.

- *Do I have a regimen to ensure my meetings deliver great outcomes?*
- *How would others rate the value I bring into meetings?*

For(give)ness is the power that is needed for giving.

During the course of our lifetime we will ask forgiveness hundreds, if not thousands, of times, and justifiably so. There will also be times that we won't ask but should. Then there are the times we will have an opportunity to forgive someone who offends, betrays, or hurts us, and sometimes we'll forgive them and sometimes we won't.

Forgiveness is a selective activity, but it shouldn't be. There is a maturity in forgiving others that comes from understanding how fragile and volatile we all are as humans. The fact that we forgive some things and don't forgive others is simply because we choose not to walk a few feet in someone else's shoes.

But if we can't naturally reach that level of sensitivity, then a good starting point would be to note the word *give* in forgiveness. It implies that in order to for*give* someone, we must take something away from ourselves; things like bitterness, resentment, hostility, and perhaps the idea of using the offense as a weapon (you know, those little digs or the common "but you did xyz"). Temporary forgiveness is nothing more than manipulation, but to truly forgive is to never bring it up again . . . ever!

The grander opportunity rests in giving up offenses completely to wind up free from their bondage on our heart, mind, and spirit. The stress and anxiety of holding on to unforgiveness is nowhere as taxing as the effort it takes to forgive. Let's face it, on our deathbed, nobody's offenses will matter anyway, and holding on to those offenses will only get us there that much sooner.

Realize the power and peace you will acquire through forgiveness today!

- *Will I develop my strength to be giving vs. taking when someone offends me?*
- *Who in my life do I need to forgive, and how will I go about this?*

In everyone's life, there are pages that are simply a must-read.

The world is full of amazing, weird, abrasive, gentle, controlling, unusual, serious, creative, rigid, casual, analytical, esoteric, strange, intense, and yes, even bizarre people. Yet there is a beauty in everyone waiting to be discovered based on our commitment to do a little digging, regardless of their personality. But oftentimes, we avoid people; we judge them based on what we see, hear, or feel, because it's easier to judge them than it is to engage them. Unfortunately, this posture not only eliminates great opportunities to enhance our social skills, it causes us to miss out on the gems that can make every encounter worth a little extra effort.

You've heard the old saying, "You can't judge a book by its cover." Well, people are much the same way, only there are a lot more pages to access. But until we read a few pages of their life, we won't know much, let alone the whole picture, will we? Yet we tend to put people in a box. We throw their book away or put it aside as we look at them through our own lens of how they feel to us, not what is possible through us. Intermittently, we ignore our capacity to draw out the beauty in people—their story, their life, their value—and as a result both people miss the possibility of who knows what.

The true genius in relationships is one who shows interest in others, and whether cursory or comprehensive, does so knowing that everyone can be a book worth reading.

Read a few lines of someone's life today. It may be a lifeline for you.

- *Do I discard people who don't fit my perfect social profile?*
- *Do I have a desire to improve my social skills with all people or just some?*

Consider your personal mission statement— the shorter, the better.

As a mission, vision, and values developer, my charge has always been to commandeer over-homogenized, uninspiring, forgettable corporate mission statements and reduce them down to a single, powerful sentence to be remembered, to inspire and drive into life. Through research, I've discovered that if mission statements cannot be remembered, the results are catastrophic . . . like forgetting an anniversary or a birthday. So crafting corporate mission statements into compelling, easy to remember, and realistic to execute lines is essential to future prosperity. Personal mission statements are no different, but rarely do we take the time to craft out who we will be, what we will stand for, and how we will infuse our own special contribution into the world. Personal mission statements are just that—*personal*. Mine, for example, is based on my passion to bring perspective to things that hinder possibility in relationships, business, and life. So my personal mission statement, based on my style of engagement, is "To be a graceful interruption to whatever is not working in someone's life."

Consider a few things when developing your mission statement. First, make the statement a way of being so it can span all areas of your life, and avoid making it a role or duty, as that is limiting to the mission. Next, make sure it has enough inspiration to create the passion that is needed to make it last a lifetime. This generally happens when you link your mission statement to your unique gifting and ability. Make it a mission that affects the lives of other people. Missions are cause-based and about the need to make a difference with others. Lastly, give the line a cool factor and a nice cadence so you'll feel good *saying it*, and feel even better *doing it*.

Develop your own personal mission statement today!

- *What if I lived every day with a clear mission in all areas of life?*
- *Will I start the process of developing my personal mission statement?*

It's best when the pages of the books you read align to serve the pages of your life.

Many people like to read, but the relevancy of what people read always confounds me. It seems there is rarely a correlation between what is going on in someone's life and what they are reading. So rather than reading material that *impacts* current circumstances, people often read to *escape* from current circumstances. Not that reading for entertainment should be frowned upon, but there are always things we need to be schooled up on, and it might be wise to consider reading on *those* things before escaping into some form of fiction—a novel idea, I know.

Case in point: I was once counseling someone whose marriage was in serious trouble. So I asked what he was reading these days, and he replied, "A book on the end of the world." I replied, "It sounds like we should be less concerned about the end of the world and more concerned about the end of your marriage, don't you think?" *The Five Love Languages* followed by *Us* quickly became the reading of the day.

Because most reading comes from the latest and greatest book trend or a recommendation from a friend, relative, or associate, 90 percent of the time what people are reading has nothing to do with what *their* struggle is in life. And yet there are always struggles. We all have areas in our lives where we need healing or would like to grow. But rather than prioritizing *these* areas with focus and intentionality, we read unrelated content while the specific learning we need for growth sits on a shelf somewhere, and we end up reading what's *current*, not what's *relevant*.

To stay on a journey of learning in key areas of urgency and not get distracted into the latest and greatest is a discipline that will reap amazing dividends of growth where it matters most.

Pages don't always mean progress. Consider reading what is critical today.

• *Is what I am reading a value-add to my life or an escape from it?*
• *What one topic could I benefit from learning about?*

Believe it or not, you have superhuman powers to extend your life. Get up an hour earlier tomorrow.

Ask most people these days about critical needs, and most who are busy will tell you they could use more time. But to my knowledge, the time machine isn't available for purchase just yet, and any attempts to change a day from 24 hours to say . . . 36 have not been embraced, nor would they be effective, as time is finite no matter how we do the math.

Yet the truth is in—we *all* want more time: more time to live, more time to love and appreciate life, and more time to get more done. So what's the answer to the age-old question of leveraging and stretching time? It's simple—alarm clocks, available at your local drugstore for the price of a couple triple venti lattes. And what's alarming is that people don't take advantage of this cheap, simple, and dependable life-changing "life extension technology." Just an hour earlier every day creates 365 hours a year, 3,650 over a decade, and 9,125 over 25 years. There, you just added over a year to your life. Get up two hours earlier and you add two years to your life productivity.

What could you do with an extra year or two of time? The possibilities are endless, and there's something very special about early morning time. For some reason it moves slower than day or nighttime. It's calmer and is an amazing time to plan out the craziness ahead and bring perspectives for the day that will make things work better and more effectively at every turn. And a day gone well will generally facilitate a better night's sleep. Do you really need that extra hour of sleep? I'll let you decide. Could you use that extra hour in your day? In these times, we all could.

Time to activate the alarm clock.
Time to activate your ambitions.

- *Could I remove stress from my day if I spent time to prepare for the day?*
- *What would I do if I had that extra hour every day?*

What you *eat* can determine how clearly and effectively you *think*.

I've always felt that the school system would benefit tremendously, as would those who attend school, if food and its effects on mood, behavior, and physical and mental performance were a required class . . . every year. Kids would have a better life and better grades, and teachers would have more alert, focused students. Well, life goes on, we become adults, and although we've picked up a little hearsay, watched a few TV shows, and read an article or two on health, most haven't had enough exposure to the hard truths of diet and the impact that food has on life.

Truth is, every physical body has eating realities that determine how well it performs. But most don't know the basics, let alone the formula that will work for their individual bodies. We were never taught that we are unique and that the Standard American Diet falls short. Fact is, there is nothing standard about our blood type, DNA, physical makeup, medical history, or family history.

And yet we're presented with a one-size-fits-all diet. Quite a blunder, if you ask me. Lethargy, mental cloudiness, lack of focus, fatigue, and depression can all be reduced, if not eliminated, if we discover what we need to put into, and remove out of, our diet. Every human body has a formula for optimum mental and physical performance, and it pays to discover what that is. Fortunately, there is infinite information on the subject, including books, web content, and seminars that explain eating for your blood, body, and metabolic type. The good news is that the return on investment of a little time and commitment should be notable in the first week or two.

Discover what your high-performance food intake is today.

- *Have I ever considered that what I eat is a key to maximizing productivity?*
- *Will I pay attention to how I feel after certain meals so I can tune my intake?*

Those who say, "You can't change the world," actually change it every day.

Too many people live life in the skeptic tank. With their pessimism and negative attitude, casually or seriously negative people bring a little hopelessness every day to those around them. Even without words, one's mere posture of pessimism can have a polarizing effect on people, projects, and progress.

As you know, we live in a world with no shortage of perspectives from billions of people, millions of websites, hundreds of TV channels, thousands of radio stations, and books—too many to count. Perspectives abound. Some of them inspire us, some say nothing, and some have the ability to rain on our parade for a while. Pessimism is an *art-form* for some, but it's really more of a *heart-storm* for all who are in its ugly presence. It can show up in a glance, in an attitude, in our words, in our actions, and in our body language. Pessimism can be subtle, almost clandestine, as our attitude is always on and is capable of delivering negativity at will.

It's wise to note that at any given moment we're either being optimistic, pessimistic, or neutral. Neutral people, although better than pessimists, have a negative impact also, because an uncommitted stance inspires no one, and over time it will sabotage possibility. Pessimists leave their stain on all things. The only worthwhile posture to have is optimism.

Be the optimist in your world today.

• *Do I lean more toward optimism or cynicism in my life?*
• *In what areas or with whom could I use an attitude adjustment?*

Don't confuse being a visionary with the ability to bring forth a vision.

Ideas are easy. Many come from out of nowhere, and for some people, new ones hit with amazing frequency. In fact, there are more super successful, *unrealized* ideas floating around than we think. You probably have a few great ones you've been toying with for a while, perhaps for a lifetime. But the execution of those ideas is another story altogether. Most innovations fail due to lack of focus, discipline, and commitment. I call it medicating one's self with distractions, avoiding the work and sacrifice it takes to turn a single idea into an actual success story.

To be a relevant visionary means bringing at least one idea to full maturity so other ideas that follow have a clear and sustainable path to success. Much of the innovation needed to bring an idea to fruition is procured along the journey of turning the idea into a reality. It's in this process that ideas become better, our character stronger, and our skills and abilities empowered in ways we can't fathom. In contrast, ideas worked to a point, then abandoned, will reduce our confidence and resources, and will denigrate our reputation with others a few notches. The value that exists in bringing an idea to maturity goes beyond the success it brings; it makes us more capable people and strengthens our influence, credibility, and future opportunity.

Blow the dust off one of your ideas and bring it into reality today.

- *Of all my ideas, which would be the most profitable and enjoyable to work on?*
- *Are there others I can get counsel from who've turned ideas into success?*

To be anxious is to wait longer.

Back in the day, perhaps a few thousand years ago, I'd guess that lines were a bit shorter, traffic wasn't as bad, and the urgency to get places was relegated to the pace of a horse, not horsepower. This to say that patience was probably in greater supply in those days.

Today, life is all about speed, and as for patience, it is a rare and elusive trait. With the population growing, traffic increasing, and lines the norm, waiting is a given. But no matter how much time you have to wait for something or someone, the *choice* to be impatient means you will wait even longer—not physically, but where it matters most . . . emotionally. Engaging in a bit of mental gymnastics can go a long way in shortening the emotional duration of anything you wait for; and if you think about it, you have to wait for *everything*, even the next split second. The decision to ensure that time adds value and reduces anxiety requires managing how we relate to time and the events therein. It's a life-management decision we can make, stick in our mental pocket, and take with us for the rest of our lives.

So if impatience is causing consistent anxiety, it would be wise to understand that having patience is to create less of a wait, create more opportunity, and extend more of our life . . . perhaps literally.

We can't control the wait time, just the anticipate time!

- *Is an impatient disposition worth the imposition?*
- *What are the areas in my life where I always feel impatient?*

Failure has the ability to take me from being a complete idiot to being less of an idiot . . . almost overnight.

Effort x Failure = Just about anything you want!

It all started in school. Pass or fail. "Pass" meant you were safe until the next test; "fail" meant that going home was an experience you'd rather not relive. "Fail" also left us to entertain an inventory of self-judgments ranging from "I'm an idiot" to "I'll never make it" to "I don't really care"—all lies, all the wrong perspective.

The reason for this common view of failure is that the value in failing is something few people are equipped to talk about, mainly because they hold their own failures as a failure. Failure is nothing more than a unique opportunity to become a better, more aware human being. So rather than taking months, years, or a lifetime to get over a failure, our reaction should be to have grace on ourselves, learn and grow through the experience, and get on with the next thing within hours or days, not months or years.

Through a series of my own failures, I've come to learn that taking chances and risking failure is a genius strategy for ensuring success. "Fail away," I say. According to some executives, a venture risked, then failed, can have the value equivalent to a master's degree for those who maintain a teachable posture in the process. And as a learning mechanism, failure does one thing that education can't always do: it creates an emotional, as opposed to cerebral, connection to transformation that is rarely forgotten.

Go for it today, whether you think you'll fail or not!

- Is how I view failure sabotaging my future potential?
- Have I considered that successful people have had more failures than successes?

Offense has no aim—it just happens to hit whoever exposes its despair.

You've heard the phrases "They attacked me personally" or "That was personal." But what if there was no such thing as a personal attack of any kind? For one, we would stop taking any offense personally and could rest in the fact that these attacks really have nothing to do with us, even though we may feel like the intended target. It shows maturity to resist feelings of being personally attacked, betrayed, or offended. It's advanced-level wisdom to accept that it's impossible for something to be directed solely at us. Our capacity to withstand the onslaught of assaults will strengthen as we resist them.

Claiming an attack to be "personal" is an illusion and a form of self-flattery that we're somehow important enough for someone to directly invest their hatred and undone stuff into us. Personal attacks really have nothing to do with us, but everything to do with someone who is simply working out their issues, and in some cases . . . their attacks land on us. We just happen to be the ones in their line of fire from time to time. Trust me, when you feel attacked, there are others who are also reaping the whirlwind of the same unresolved issues, showing how these breakdowns are completely impersonal, random by-products of the attacker's inner problems. The peace that comes with acknowledging the impersonal nature of attacks, no matter how personal they look, removes confusion, adds compassion, and multiplies our strength to help others through their issues.

Don't take offense at other people's troubles today. Their attacks are not really aimed at you.

- *Will I be more at peace in life if I view offenses as personal or impersonal?*
- *Who is an offensive person I can practice being at peace with?*

Encouragement has the unique ability to improve everything in a matter of seconds.

If you've ever been down—and you have, many times—you'll connect to the value that encouragement has added in the quality, effectiveness, and growth in your life. It can be the ingredient that transforms hopelessness or discouragement into optimism and courage, and it can do so instantly. It can be the catalyst that can take a downward spiral—real or imagined—stop it, and reverse the process no matter how big the circumstances or how intense the problems.

Whether we are a mom, dad, employee, pastor, or CEO, we can all stand to have people in our lives who encourage us when life twists an ugly turn. But knowing the real meaning behind encouragement is the beginning of being able to give it as well as receive it. Simply put, *encouragement* means "to deposit courage into someone." With a little bit of commitment, a few discerning words, and a bit of *courage* on our part, we have an amazing capacity to *deposit courage* into people. Affirming their gifts, accomplishments, ability to do the job before them, and noting the difference they make are just the start. Everyone has their own spin on encouragement. The key is to implement it and then measure the effectiveness of your encouragement by seeing what actually happens through your efforts. Does your encouragement move people to act, or just to nod, smile, and say a polite "thank you"? Courage is as courage ultimately does.

Get a little courage and give a little courage today.

- *Am I a source for bringing courage to others, or am I mute or even discouraging?*
- *Who in my life right now could use a bit of encouragement?*

No conversation is complete without a conversational risk.

There is no such thing as a boring conversation; there are only bored people who integrate their boredom into conversations, as well as other areas of life. Let's face it, conversational complacency is commonplace today. The empty pleasantries of dancing on the surface of people's lives seem the norm when real richness exists in engaging at a deeper, more intimate level. Discovering what is really going on with people is the beginning of relationship, and it can be done without being obtrusive simply by asking great questions—ones that challenge, open up, and reveal what is real for a person.

For example, when I talk with strangers, I won't ask the standard question, "How are you today?" because what I will get back will be a stock answer designed to end the conversation or cover up what is really going on. You will find me asking, "So what is your vision in life?" or "What are you passionate about?" or "If you could do anything and not fail, what would you do?" They always look puzzled and a bit intrigued at first, but often they start talking openly about their life, and what could have been a go-nowhere wordplay turns into a legitimate conversation. Although it's just a few minutes of dialogue, I get to encourage them in their vision, passion, or dream, and I make a new friend in the process. The key is to become expert at inquiry.

Take some time to engineer a series of thought-provoking questions that inspire communication rather than shut it down and you'll have discovered the secret to drawing out what is amazing in people—all people.

Take your conversations to a deeper level, not a sleeper level, today.

- *Am I more about keeping peace or contributing value during conversations?*
- *Will I begin to move conversations to more depth and meaning?*

Take care of others; the rest will take care of itself.

The value in serving others is that we get value in the process . . . often more than we give.

I know the process and discipline to count others as more important than ourselves is a tough one to swallow, especially when we don't see immediate returns, appreciation, or reciprocation from others. But giving of ourselves on that level has little to do with what we get from others and is more about the blessing we bestow on ourselves . . . by giving of ourselves. Those who sow well in life are rarely in lack of being fulfilled, and those who take the time to care for others and do it from a truly authentic disposition generally reap a variety of benefits, including gratitude, favor, and priority, all of which are worth the choice to be more about others than ourselves.

One thing is certain: Every measure of peace, joy, and prosperity in relationships is dependent on our commitment to serve others and create value for them. Whether business associates, family, friends, or even strangers, bringing value to others has a unique way of coming back to us in multiples. It's not always instant, which stops many a visionless giver. But those with long-sighted thinking know that when they wake up, they either contribute something into the world that day or take something out of it. They're clear that the result of giving is much more rewarding than living in a taking posture any day of the week.

Who is in need of your unique ability to care today?

- *How often do I consciously count others as more important than myself?*
- *What could one day of serving others before myself turn into?*

Thinking about your life
from the end of it backward
is *truly* forward thinking.

The most valuable of our life senses is the sense of life urgency.

I remember once when I was asked to write my own epitaph. An odd request, but amused and intrigued, I indulged. For the moment, the exercise of putting finiteness on my life forced me to think with a sense of urgency and clarity, not the day-to-day vagueness I often live in. Being more of a visionary than a planning type, I always envisioned there was no need for urgency and figured, *Who needs the stress now? I'll put it off until later.* Now that a few years—OK, decades—have passed, I call my youthful thinking the trap of "I've got boatloads of time." Actually, we don't. Time is like rust; momentum builds as time goes on. The foresight of realizing how short life is should force everyone to put a little more effort into seeing into the later years. There is great value in thinking through the details of our total life picture and working toward the ends we desire. When we take the time to see what's really achievable in the time we have left, it will sober us right up to what we'll need to do in the present time to have the future turn out the way we envision. This is the true beginning of a great ending. Or one day, you'll wake up and realize the years left simply can't add up to what you thought and dreamed about. The clock is ticking. . . .

Spend some time thinking about the later years—today.

- *Do I live frivolously, as if there's endless time available?*
- *Will I spend time thinking about the time I have left and what I desire from it?*

It's never the conflict,
but what's underneath the conflict that matters.

We could all use a little less conflict in our lives, but one could argue that!

Conflicts are often a mystery. They're a puzzle, and the solution isn't always so obvious. Neither is figuring out what caused them so they don't happen again. The endless number of circumstances and moods we experience make it difficult to tell when something will set us off. Unfortunately, we are driven by our feelings so much of the time that our understanding of conflict is not based on root causes but on our mood—how we feel at a given moment in time—making it difficult to get past the feelings into revelation and healing. Often we miss the real cause and end up putting a Band-Aid on the emotion for the moment, hoping the pain will go away, but it doesn't. Those same emotions will resurface in short order only to cause stronger resentment and frustration each time the conflict occurs—all because Band-Aids are easier to apply than a commitment to explore the root cause. And yes . . . there *is* always a root cause to be found.

For example, when one of my employees isn't performing up to my expectations and it becomes a conflict, is the conflict about my own disappointment that I didn't get what I wanted, or is it because I haven't trained that employee, inspired them with vision, and supported them with the tools they need to succeed? Or did the employee just lose a relative, or are they having problems at home? If we ever want to reduce conflicts, we should learn to embrace them, improve our skills in dealing with them, and learn to get to the bottom of them no matter who's at fault.

Look past the conflict into what's really going on today.

- *Is it my tendency to sweep conflicts under the rug, hoping they will go away?*
- *Are there recurring conflicts where the root cause remains undiscovered?*

If you put the right heads together, you'll come up with one incredibly brilliant brain.

It's either T.E.A.M.—Together Everyone Accomplishes More, or T.E.A.M.—Together Everyone's A Moron.

It's quite strange, but the older we get, the more we realize how much we don't know. Although we grow wiser with every day, we also become more aware of our ignorance, and that superhero mentality—I can do it all, I know it all—is a thing of the past, just like our admiration for superheroes. In today's world, leveraged mindshare is the name of the game. Real intelligence isn't born out of an "if it is to be, it is up to me" attitude; it comes from assembling the right team of minds, hearts, and hands to get a job done. Superhuman intelligence is about doing advance work to make sure the team that is at the table will be exponentially more powerful than the total head count at the table. But teamwork is a liability if it's not the *right* team. If there is a breakdown in the assembly, it will be much like a complex machine being assembled with parts that don't belong and without parts that are critical. The result is failure by design.

Effective brain-trust is never about the quantity of heads but the quality of heads at the table. It's about considering gift sets, experiences, personalities, commitment levels, passions, track records, and many other details that are unique to each initiative. Ignoring these details causes strife, competition, chaos, and the quick demise of a team that should never have been fused. It only takes one bad apple in a meeting to polarize a room. Assembling the right team is in the discernment and care it takes to do it well, and if you think about it, the largest, most successful organizations in the world are comprised of one big, well-thought-out team.

Pick your team members with great care today.

- *Is my team selection process based more on comfort or wisdom?*
- *What needs to get done that could get done if the right team were in place?*

Never underestimate the gift of a single smile . . . for others and for you.

Smiles. It seems I never get tired of them. No matter who they come from, smiles change something inside of me that I can't quite understand, nor do I want to. Smiling just feels good. In fact, stop reading right now and smile for five seconds (see what I mean?).

Aside from the fact that a single smile releases positive mood-enhancing chemicals in the brain called endorphins and removes stress-enhancing chemicals such as dopamine, cortisol, and adrenaline, smiles are contagious and can bring a smile to others' faces. Ultrasounds have shown we smile when we're in the womb; we also smile when we're asleep as babies, and we smile more as kids than we do as adults. So somewhere along the course of our lives (perhaps one Clint Eastwood Western too many), smiling became not so cool anymore, and thus CSDS ensued—Controlled Smile Disorder Syndrome.

Regardless of the psychology of it all, smiling and creating smiles are among the most underutilized assets we have as human beings. Smiles are contagious both in business and in social circumstances, and smiles position us to be more desirable. They have been proven to make us appear more confident and competent than those who don't smile. There are even correlations between smiling and longevity. Given the stress-reducing and joy-inducing properties of smiling, it both makes sense and brings delight to our senses. That alone should give us something to smile about. ☺

Smile a bit more and stress a bit less today.

• *Have I taken a moment to contemplate the things I have to smile about?*
• *Is there room for more smiles in my life? Who in my life could use more smiles?*

A weakness is often a strength that went too far.

Weaknesses are not nearly as damaging as strengths that fall out of governance!

If you take a close look at what causes problems in your life, you may discover it's not your weaknesses that are the reason for your troubles. It sounds odd, but all of our strengths are a two-way street that can be the road to prosperity or the road to a dead end. Our strengths can be effective in making great progress and growth where we want, and they can flip over into immaturities that can do great damage with relationships in every area of our life. But how is it that strengths can create such grief? One with the gift of control, for example, might manage things well, but can easily become a control freak by micromanaging people and processes. Great analytical minds can over-think themselves into analysis paralysis. Those with the strength of communication can talk too much. The strength of caring for others can go too far and ignore one's own basic needs. The strength of discernment can move to indifference and judgment. The strength of being a great debater can spur one to argue at every turn. The strength of placing value on relationships can move to holding relationships as idols, breeding codependency. The strength of doing well can move to anxiety-filled perfectionism.

The strength of being a follower can alienate opportunities to lead. Bottom line: Keep an eye on the strengths you have, as they are dangerous and damaging when they go too far.

**Today, ask yourself if your strengths
are bringing life or creating strife.**

- *What are my top strengths? Read* StrengthsFinder 2.0 *to learn more.*
- *How can my strengths go too far and cause problems?*

Follow your heart. It's smarter than you think.

eart vs. Head. Let's get ready to rumble!!!
No battle in the history of humankind has persisted with more intensity and duration than the internal battle of intellect vs. emotion / thinking vs. feeling. We've all heard "You should have gone with your heart," and we've also heard "You should have used your head." There is no "perfect" formula for predicting outcomes, whether you use your head or your heart. But the heart, the gut, the instinct—whatever you call it—is that innate thing you know defines the true you in the midst of decision. It goes against the grain of the "needing others' approval, not wanting to make a mistake" stigma that throws us into a tentative, dispassionate state of mind. Going with our heart also pulls us out of recycled thinking and allows the freedom to feel through our decisions into a driving force that is more sustainable than any other force—and that is *passion*.

So what's the upside of following your heart? If you succeed, which you'll do more often, you'll confirm the approach and experience more joy, and life will have more depth, meaning, and fulfillment. If you fail, you'll learn from it, only to go with your heart and a bit more wisdom on the next go-around. Not to backpedal, but if the heart is really into something you're desiring, it will not only consult the head, it will also seek the advice of others to give your vision the highest chance of success. Using your heart is never an excuse to throw your head in the drawer.

Go with your heart, and head in the right direction today.

• *Do I typically follow my heart or head?*
• *Have I ever stopped to think that I can be led by both, with one being primary?*

Mind over madder.

Prolonged anger will do nothing more than drive you mad.

The inner turmoil of a mad person is seldom overt or publicly visible. You rarely ever see someone walking around with a scrunched-up scowl on their face, stomping down the street, snapping at bystanders in a fit of rage. Anger is much more subversive than that. Anger generally manifests in an inner tone that lies in wait for something to set it off, to offend it. Depending on the level of the anger or the circumstances, the explosion of an inner tone of anger can be damaging beyond repair.

In contrast, anger expressed in small doses that don't convert to tantrum tidal waves is not unhealthy at all. In fact, anger isn't a bad emotion, but if it builds up over time, it will cloud thinking so severely that we'll lose all reason and all reasons to deal with the issues at hand, and our emotional vents will shut and the heat will store up.

Let's face it, anger happens, and in quick release with a touch of restraint it is healthy. But holding on to anger is our choice, and when we let it build, anger will store in the body just like fat does. That's where angry people come from. They hold on to anger, and when the moment hits, it manifests in the ugly words and actions that will later be regretted. The idea that we can get angry, parse it out in small bits, and get past it makes it a learned skill to keep all rooms cool, calm, and collected—especially the room for improvement.

**Releasing anger in small doses
will largely reduce our stress levels.**

- *Do I deal with my anger and frustrations or do I suppress them?*
- *Have I considered how I can express my anger without hurting others?*

Waiting in line is not an annoyance . . .
it's potential!

The best line is the one that's a smile long.

There are many things that slow our momentum in life. Waiting for someone to finish using the bathroom are the number one and number two culprits (sorry). And then there's waiting in lines—the DMV, Starbucks, concerts, clubs, sporting events—and the list grows on . . . as do the lines. Whatever the delay, there are opportunities that exist in all of our wait time that can *create* momentum and progress, not stop them. Historically accurate, here are just a few of the millions of amazing outcomes that can result from someone who is committed to taking advantage of a long wait in line: new client acquisition, marriage, multimillion-dollar deals, deep friendships, plus new resources, vendors, movie tips, and more.

Unfortunately, in some cases a line that moves too quickly can cut short an opportunity to create a valuable connection. Despite the size and speed of a line, there is relational, emotional, or financial gold there to be had. Think about it: Your audience is captive, they can't get away from you, they're bored stiff and perhaps willing to talk. The question is who will start? I've got news for you: They won't. People today are pretty shut down to opening up conversations, but most are willing to talk if *you* start one. You never know where it may lead. You may score big or go bust. But one thing is certain: Lines move a lot quicker when you're talking instead of staring or succumbing to frustration.

Striking up a conversation in line will have things looking up today.

- *What are some conversation starters to start maximizing my time in lines?*
- *Will I ever look at lines the same way again?*

Wisdom is saying enough to prove your point, not your existence.

S ometimes the absence of words can be the key to more effective communication.

My wife told me recently that I would be more effective in my life if I showed a "little" more conversational restraint. I think what she was saying so diplomatically was the more I talked, the more I could come across as a know-it-all, and she was spot on. I took her words to heart as coaching, not reprimand. I realized that if I listened a little more, processed what was said with more care and attention, and waited for the "more opportune moments" to speak, conversations would be less about my wanting to be acknowledged as a great communicator and more about creating trust, efficiency, and effectiveness in relationships. It was life-changing for me, and I'm grateful she had the courage to share it.

Not sure if you've ever read it, but there is limitless wisdom to be found in the Bible, and there's a verse in Ecclesiastes that reads, "The more the words, the less the meaning, and how does that profit anyone?" (Eccles. 6:11). What it's saying is that we have a tendency to say too much. It implies that if we are communicating with wisdom, we won't waste words but will say what needs to be said in a focused, concise, and sensitive manner. With a new commitment to brevity, I now know the truth can be said with optimum strength in a single sentence, and it doesn't require exaggerations, exhaustive details, or our need to sound off to make the point. Fewer words, more dialogue, better understanding, and less drama are just a few of the benefits of staying out of the bloviating zone. This being said, I think I'll say no more.

Offer poignant, less verbose statements today, and see how much more gets said ... and done!

- *Do I take into account the value of time and productivity in my conversations?*
- *Can I make my points more effectively with "laser-like" communication?*

Stress* is a *choice*!

Stress will make us older but not always wiser. Consider that everything we do, good or bad, has value to us, and we do it because there is a payoff of some sort; otherwise, we wouldn't do it. Stress is no different. Some people *choose* to allow stress to occur, simply so they can feel alive. Others choose not to deal with stress by postponing it, causing more stress. Still others choose to turn stress into unproductivity as a strategy for complacency, as a way to get out of work. It's as if the difficulty of stressing out is somehow easier than the stress of working, focusing, and developing. Granted, the occurrences of life are unpredictable, and stress will show up whether we like it or not. But how we deal with stress will always come down to choice. There are books to read, prayers if you pray, advisers to consult, exercise to be done, deep breathing to engage in, the right foods to eat. The list of stress-reducing options is endless, as are the disciplines to deal with and reduce the effects of stress.

The mind is a habit machine that frames up life and our reaction to circumstances in two modes: default or choice. *Default* typically looks like checking out, numbing out, and stressing out. *Choice* looks like checking in, thinking on, talking through, or getting help. The moment you begin the process of choice in your stress is the moment stress begins to lose its power.

Choose not to stress today.

- *When stress hits, is my first instinct to succumb to it or contend with it?*
- *What are some of the ways I can deal with stress when it comes?*

*The stress I'm referring to in this ShiftPoint is the day-to-day stress we deal with. Death, disease, and serious tragedy are in a different category and get a temporary pass but are always helped by moving to choice rather than defaulting to stress.

If you're going to be a real player in life, it would help to be clear on the various levels of commitment.

Ahhhh, the report cards. They never go away!

Everything is at a level. Any level-headed person knows that, depending on their level. Water in a glass has a level, skill sets have a level, relationships are at a level, world peace is at a level, and of course our commitments are at a level. At any given moment, everything is at some level of fullness or emptiness, and it's rare that we check in to see what those levels are, because we're just too busy doing life. But there is tremendous benefit in doing quick evaluations from time to time based on the premise that there are four levels of commitment.

You are operating in one of them in all areas of your life right now. They are as follows: (1) *Playing to lose.* The commitment to do nothing, to sit on the sidelines and watch life pass by, where complacency is valued more than progress and comfort more than discipline. (2) *Playing not to lose.* Doing just enough to get by, but not taking any risks and being so careful that nothing really good or bad ever happens to you . . . a tentative existence. (3) *Playing to play.* Not a bad place to be, but you are always in jeopardy of falling back on *playing not to lose*, as you never really get ahead in this zone of play. (4) *Playing to win.* This fourth level is the only one that ensures progress. It embraces challenges, ignores feelings and obstacles, and knows whatever price one has to pay to have something turn out is nothing compared to the price of complacency. This level gives the pain a purpose and makes the discomfort of growth almost pleasurable. It ensures the success of our goals and ourselves at every level of our life.

What level of commitment will you play at today?

- *When was the last time I did a "level" check in the various areas of my life?*
- *What level is lowest at this time, and what level must I play at to change that?*

Vulner(ability)

Truth is the beginning of the end for all strongholds.

As humans, one of the scarier things in life is to be fully honest with how we think, feel, and process life. Unfortunately, the misconception that others can't be trusted with our vulnerability has more to do with our own insecurities than it does distrust of others. As for the impact of keeping this stuff inside—it creates enough baggage to weigh heavy on the strongest of minds, if not completely incapacitate them.

I can relate to this. At a restaurant many years ago, I confessed to my wife, "Honey, I'm a poser. I've got so many façades, I can't keep them straight." I didn't maintain these façades for malicious or manipulative reasons. I kept the plastic alive because I felt inadequate, comparing myself to anyone I thought was better than me, and keeping the veneer in place was more about survival than anything else. After a long talk and a good steak, she recommended that I reach out and share with my trusted friends what was real for me in my life. One conversation after the next, I shared openly about my issues, fears, and thought life. I listened, I even cried at times, and in six short months, the need to be noticed, the need for attention, and the need for façades reduced themselves to near nothing. Other people went from being threats to being friends seemingly overnight, and in the process, they began to open up to me about *their* issues. I heard statements after my sharing like, "Well, Dean, you think that's bad . . ." or "That's all you got?" It opened up a world of truth, and through others' sharing their stuff with me, I discovered I had a knack for coaching and counseling. It's amazing what can come from sharing the fullness of our truths.

There is tremendous "ability" in vulnerability. Consider a conversational risk today!

- *When was the last time I became vulnerable and shed some emotional weight?*
- *Who can I trust to discuss these issues with and when will I start?*

In a world of texting, emailing, and social networking, basic social skills are virtually dying.

The basic human bond we share is more personal than pixels. The internet, for all its value and resources, is instrumental in breaking down the basic social solidarity of the human race. Not that it was intended that way, nor is it totally at fault, but when you provide channels of communication that "virtually replace" a bulk of human contact via the phone or face-to-face, you end up with a society accustomed to communicating without physical or voice contact. The danger is that technology will make it so easy to communicate, as well as control incoming communications, that the communication of choice will be that of buttons and keystrokes rather than mouths, eyes, and facial expressions.

You can decide whether or not this is having an effect on relational intimacy by simply walking down the street and noticing the disposition of those around you. I mean, really *look*. You'll be astonished at what you see if you pay attention long enough. Are most people friendly, open to a verbal exchange, eye contact, or a simple nod? Or do you see people becoming increasingly self-protective, reserved, emotionally roped off, iPod/iPad addicted, lost in texting? Now look at your own disposition, more specifically your own personal commitment to break through technological and social reclusion and engage at a more intimate level. This is where the opportunity lies. Repeat after me: "It's amazing how much more engaged others have become with me since I've become more engaged with them."

Break down barriers of social reclusion today.

- *How much of my people interaction has been replaced with pixel interaction?*
- *Am I content with my basic social skills, or would I like them to be stronger?*

Never underestimate the power of who will do what by when.

When you're vague, you're the plague. Your lack of clarity spreads like the disease that it is.

It suffices to say that when an icon like Jack Welch, formerly of General Electric, writes that one of the biggest breakdowns in business is lack of candor, what he's referring to is a gross shortage of honest, clear, and specific communication during typical day-to-day business interactions. Call it what you like, 90 percent of all organizations suffer from lack of straightforward communication, and one form is called "the daily mystery of who will do what by when." For whatever reason, leaving out the critical details during task-based communication has become standard operating procedure, because for the moment, it always seems easier to be casual rather than detailed, hoping others will fill in the gaps. Actually, that's the moment confusion begins and potential stops.

I know it seems basic: Who and What by When. But business depends on momentum, and the one thing companies and individuals can't afford to lose in today's business environment is momentum. The constant starts and stops that come from not knowing the details of Who, What, and When takes all the fun out of business . . . as well as the potential.

The interesting part is that specificity in communication is not so much about what you have to do—it's about who you are. It's living in a discipline of being a clear person. You develop your character and your way of being with people while measuring the results you attain . . . specifically! And if your results are less than adequate, you'll be willing to look at your role and take account for those results as a responsible human, not as a victim. This is the attitude of professionals, the ones who are clear about Who is going to do What by When.

- *Do I leave conversations knowing the exact next steps? Do I write them down?*
- *How much benefit would there be if there were total clarity in my interactions?*

What you think can record itself in your mind—as a real event.

Think it, be it. It's more real than we think.

The single point of processing for every perspective we have is found between our ears. The mind is command central, the processing plant everything must go through before it becomes a feeling, posture, attitude, or action. It is the hub of all things, and yet it is rumored that at best, we only use 10 percent of our brain. If that's the case, what takes place in the remaining 90 percent? Just a mystery, I guess. But if 10 percent is tops in the brain game, I'm not sure I'd ever want to meet a person who was using all of their brain. Scary would be an understatement. Regardless, the mind is an incredible tool capable of great things, at whatever percentage it is operating at. One thing rarely mentioned, though, is that the brain has the capacity to take events that we think about and record them as if they actually happened. The body then stores these thoughts, and over time they become part of our mental makeup. This is what largely determines our attitude. How's that for powerful?

The good news is that our mind is essentially software, and we can reprogram it from where it is today to something better, stronger, and more stable. But reprogramming requires dedication to paying attention to our thought life and, as dysfunctional thoughts come up, investing a moment to remodel the thought into a new paradigm that works for us, not against us. It's these small thought-restructuring moments that all add up to an amazing attitude about life and bring our 10 percent brain capacity to a high percentage of life fulfillment.

Reprogram any ineptitudes in your attitude today.

- *Do I have control of my thoughts, or do I view them as random?*
- *What is one negative, recurring thought that I feel has become part of me?*

7 percent of our conversational impact is *what we say*, 38 percent is *our tone*, and 55 percent is our *body language*.

How would you like to read minds? By learning body language, you can get pretty close. In a world of too many words, we rarely consider the words that are spoken as the end-all. In some cases, due to an individual's track record, words may have no resonance other than a noise, lacking the credibility to even be registered as communication. Unconsciously, our natural inclination is to look past the words to determine the sincerity of the content. Perhaps we'd get more value if we were conscious about it. Not that everyone needs to be cynical or skeptical, but the older we get, the less words mean. And the reason for that is simple: By the time we hit middle age, we've experienced enough lies and broken promises to have us look at words as nothing more than a gamble. It seems the only responsible way we take notice of what others say is found in their passion, conviction, and care for us when they're speaking. It's not the *words* but a person's *way of being* that makes the communication worth the time.

In order for us to be effective communicators, our physical posture and how we say what we say will clearly reveal our intentionality and our commitment. It's always wise to "test run" our conversations in advance; put ourselves on the other side of them to experience what our communication will be like, how it will be received, and whether our physical, mental, and emotional posture is on track. The right commitment creates the right heart, stance, tone, and facial expression, otherwise known as the "total package" of communication. This is the only true way you will be able to breathe life into your words so your words will bring life to others.

Be aware of how you communicate today!

- *Do my integrity, conviction, and passion line up with the words I use?*
- *Would I benefit from being able to better discern others' sincerity and mood?*

Before you meet the who's who, you better know what's what!

During the course of our lives, we will meet people who have the capacity to accelerate our lives in extraordinary ways. It won't be often, and we'll rarely have a second chance if we miss it at the first opportunity. So it stands to reason that being a thought leader in your area of expertise is not only a wise decision, it's quite enjoyable to know more than anybody else in your area of expertise. It's an altogether different experience when you get caught not knowing what you should know. In the information age, there is no excuse for not being on the edge of what is current. The access we have to information is a keystroke or a download away, and our progress is generally proportionate to how well and how often we provide others with information that can transform their circumstances. It's the discipline of always being fresh in every meeting, conversation, and interaction that positions us for steady promotion up any corporate ladder or in any relationship.

On average, the top 5 percent of all businesspeople spend several hours a week learning various aspects of their career position, their products or services, and their industry. They not only open books and move a cursor to stay current, but they use every business activity as a learning tool and seek counsel from others on a regular basis. In short, they live a lifestyle of learning. It is this commitment that turns ordinary businesspeople into thought leaders, industry experts, and the highest-paid individuals in their category. The opportunities that come from being among the most knowledgeable players in the industry are endless.

Learn something new every day—online, in a book, or in person.

- *Will I set aside a certain amount of time to grow my knowledge base?*
- *What areas of my expertise are deficient and in need of strengthening?*

When inspiration turns to perspiration, get ready for some aviation.

There's often regret when there's not enough sweat! There seems to be a sweeping trend that hard work is no longer necessary to thrive, let alone survive. Maybe all the industrial and technological advancements that make life easier have convinced us by now that "easier" should have somehow found its way into our DNA.

But it hasn't. The human condition mandates that when it comes to making anything easier, faster, and better, it will require that humans step up to the plate and engage in serious work. This is how innovation comes alive, and I'm pretty certain that there's no shortage of innovations in the world today, just a shortage of those willing to sweat to make them become real.

In my experience, just about every person I've ever met has either had or currently has a groundbreaking idea. Human beings are inclined to innovate, impact, and influence. Unfortunately, things like fear, comfort, and skepticism get in the way of these ideas ever gaining traction. And in this entitlement age, the more we embrace the concept that the world owes us, the more we will become enslaved through debt and we'll end up owing the world. It's tragic, but most people will never put into practice the ideas they dream about because they believe that not working has more value, and that provision will always be just around the corner.

Consider that the days of provision are numbered. It's true that putting ideas into action is mentally, physically, and emotionally exhausting. However, if people realized that complacency is more painful than the commitment to put some sweat into their ideas, we'd have a much healthier, happier, and more productive world—individually and collectively.

Take an idea out of traction and put it into action today.

- *What is that vision or goal that I've been putting off for too long?*
- *Is the price of complacency worth not having the life I intended?*

A dying person has the perspective of a genius; therefore, a living person would be wise to think more like a dying person.

Have you ever contemplated what would be important to you if you were dying? One fact is true, *that day* will come for all of us. For some it will be sudden, others are given an amount of time, and for others RIP is many years down the road. Yet we have a strange aversion to death, causing us to avoid thinking about what value death could hold for us. Though it's hard to do, investing some thought about our passing may bring perspectives that would make our current lives more fulfilling and balanced. The reason we procrastinate on contemplating these things in any detail is simple: We always think we have more time . . . until of course . . . we don't.

Through a bit of due diligence, I've discovered that if you ask anyone who is dying what is important to them, they won't mention fancy cars, nice jewelry, lavish vacations, business success stories, or their last great accomplishment. And rarely will you find them protecting any façades. You will, however, find an urgency to get close to God, a refreshing authenticity, a desire to bring reconciliation to broken relationships, a commitment to share meaningful and long overdue thoughts with others, and a desire to show love in ways they never have before. The idea that these important things show up on so many deathbeds is unfortunate, because at that point, little time is left to experience the real value in the important, often-taken-for-granted areas of life—most notably immediate family, extended family, and friends. Taking your life to the end has the ability to reengineer it from "here on out." The value that comes from a small investment of thought will improve your quality of life. In fact, it may even *extend* it a bit.

Take fifteen to consider what would be important
if you were dying and live that out today.

- *Who in my life have I postponed sharing my heart with?*
- *What are the important things that could be addressed now vs. later?*

Whenever you have a meeting, make a list so you don't think twice, check back twice, or have to do it twice.

A little bit of forethought saves a lot of unnecessary afterthoughts. Lists—they seem elementary, and to some degree they are. But what's not elementary about lists is the process we go through to complete them. It's a process of considering aspects, variations, and potentials, and being thorough, complete, detailed, innovative, considerate, and productive. I'm not sure how much "elementary" I can find in those things; in fact, it sounds pretty academic. Not sure about you, but after every meeting I attend, there can be little details I missed, questions I regret not asking, and things I wished I would have covered. The more time I spend thinking about that, the more I uncover what I should have covered. So for me, I find it flattering that someone who knows me to pick their brain on occasion asks when we meet, "Hey, did ya bring the Dean's list?" I do, and I generally leave the meeting with no regrets, and rarely are things missed.

Truth is, I need the lists for a few reasons. First is my inherent need to maximize every meeting I attend down to the detail. Second, there are so many distractions and things on my mind, I find lists to be a way of ensuring my brand as a professional stays intact. Third, I respect the time of the people I'm meeting with, and I desire to lead by example so they do the same at future meetings. It really doesn't matter what the meeting entails or how many are in attendance, lists minimize stress, maximize productivity, and make things go smoother in every respect.

**If you have a meeting or important conversation,
enlist the help of a list today.**

- *How often do I leave meetings feeling I missed something?*
- *Would I consider that lists take only minutes but save hours and improve results?*

Making money is real expensive.

Everything we do has a cost—for ourselves and for others. There's always a price to pay. As we move about life, there is a constant pressure and tension to acquire enough wealth to not have to acquire wealth anymore. No shame in that. But with day-to-day goals and activities generally set around career and earning potential, "end of life" goals tend to be more important than what's right in front of us. Unfortunately, the key relationships we have in our life and how they will be affected by our quest for "that $$$ number" somehow don't make it to the front of the line. So who ultimately pays for our quest for wealth, things, and status? It's different for everyone, but generally it is those we say we care about the most who pay the most; and although it doesn't always hit us right away, *we* pay in the long run . . . a steep, relational price.

History and biographies of financially successful people show that relationships are the number one casualty of the quest for wealth. It's easy to rationalize the impact of our busyness, time away, and distracted presence because we believe we are doing something that will benefit those close to us—like attaining things, gaining financial security, or creating more time down the road. The immediate realities are that we come home late, distracted, and worst of all, we come home without the energy to focus on the needs of those around us. And then we justify it by saying, "We can fix it," when our kids don't really know us, our spouse is divorcing us in their heart, or our family and friends experience a half-connected us. It's only then we start counting the costs . . . and that's often too late.

Contemplate the costs of your goals today!

- *Am I missing precious present life because I'm absorbed by future goals?*
- *Are my family and friends getting the full me when I'm in their presence?*

Conversations that are a race instead of a pace often end in disgrace.

If you want to avoid division in relationships, give your undivided attention.

I'll address "conversations" in this book several times based on the fact that all progress in life, relationships, business, and social situations are impacted by the conversations we have and how well they turn out. There is great value in looking at the effectiveness of our conversations, including the way we listen, how we respond, and how we govern over the unpredictables that conversations bring.

I've come to learn that no matter how wise we are or how brilliant a statement we make, nothing is more brilliant in conversation than a simple, sincere response to what is being said. And nothing is more damaging to relationships than thinking of what you're going to say next, moving to your own agenda, or drifting halfway into some other thought that you think for a moment is more important than the conversation you're in. These are the traits that can turn a conversation that is riddled with potential and opportunity into a conversation that will bring an awkward parting and a poor reflection on our personal brand and reputation.

These days, with the intense pace we live in, there seems an odd pressure at times to rip through conversations rather than letting them unfold effortlessly. Removing agenda and an urgency to complete conversations creates an ease to be in them with maximum clarity and mental efficiency. It is these kinds of conversations that create the rapport and trust needed for agendas to be heard and relationships to be formed anyway. They are foundational.

Listen closely and you'll respond brilliantly today!

- *Are the conversations I have with others more life-giving or life-draining?*
- *Will I facilitate great conversations or be an ongoing victim of distracted ones?*

What ever happened to our imagination?

When I was a kid, my imagination was the key to anywhere. It opened possibilities, and the world became whatever I wanted it to be. I turned cardboard into castles, bicycles into rocket ships, trees into skyscrapers, and my third grade teacher into, well . . . let's not go there. Life then was as real as it was imaginary. There were no limits.

Then I grew up. What was once an infinite playground grew walls, confinements, and boundaries.

Somewhere during the journey of life, our imagination gets packed into a suitcase and thrown off the train, only to be replaced by cautious optimism, innovation trepidation, and imagination constipation. It is as though we were confronted with life's realities so harshly that what was once freedom into unlimited possibility became a liability. We didn't realize that we could reframe our imagination or upgrade the software to Imagination 2.0 and learn new tools, features, and nuances to apply to our current age and new stage of life. The result is that we now get caught up in the daily whirlwind, and a moment to take a deep breath for some imagination time gets suffocated by the next urgent thing.

Even as I write this, I feel a pull to give myself permission to imagine more; to slow down and combat daily urgencies so I can think freely, without reservation. Something tells me that it would be a blast, and would reveal innovation beyond my expectations and abundant possibilities for growth, all within the confines of my controlled adult life. At least that's what I imagine.

Put a little initiation into your imagination today.

- *What am I missing by not practicing the imagination of a child in my adult life?*
- *What one area of my life could use a little or a lot of imagination?*

A mirror would be more valuable if it reflected what we act like rather than what we look like.

There are few revelations greater than coming to terms with how we "actually" perform in life.

Whoever invented the mirror should have gone a bit further and created the character mirror—a mirror that goes beyond our physical looks to reveal our true character . . . good or bad. I doubt they'd sell much, unless of course they stretched the truth, flat-out lied, or reflected Pollyanna at every glance. But they'd be priceless in helping us attain perspectives for what is down inside, underneath our veneers, reflecting what we already know about ourselves but tend to conceal with great effort. Perhaps rather than images coming off the mirror, words like *giving, loving, caring, sensitive, proactive, honest, forthright, disciplined, committed* would reflect back. Or words like *taker, selfish, manipulative, arrogant, fear-driven, prideful,* and others might surface . . . or maybe a blend of the two. The main issue here is that we rarely take time to look in the character mirror, to evaluate the subtle or serious departures from integrity that we make. Fact is, we all have idiosyncrasies but would just as soon shelve them than deal with them. An equivalent to the character mirror is simply an honest look at the condition of your goals, finances, and relationships, and acting on what you can improve. Even further would be to allow others to reflect back on who you are to them for added perspective and consideration.

> **Whether through contemplation or through feedback from others, take a look in your character mirror today.**

- *When will I carve out the time to reflect on how I show up in life?*
- *Who could I ask for added perspectives? Who could be a good mirror?*

Marital problems: just another opportunity to blame something.

How neatly we label our issues so no one can hold us personally responsible! One of the most successful avoidance strategies to negate our personal responsibility in marriage is to slap a label on our issues. Marital problems, irreconcilable differences, we grew apart—you name it. Once you put a label on a marriage breakdown, the responsibility gets defrayed into a vernacular, not a person. There's no hope in that.

Frankly, I've never seen a word or a phrase stand in the gap of conflicts in marriage, only people who are committed to reconciliation and are willing to account for how they have sown, such that they have what they have. Hence the reality, there's no such thing as a marital problem. There are only individual problems and selfish behaviors we choose to bring into the marriage. The strategy to proclaim "we're having marital problems" is to skirt the consequences of our own personal contribution as whole or part of the problem and negate that responsibility. To label something takes away all of our perspective to deal with behavior and puts it conveniently in a phrase we can hide behind. How ridiculous it sounds to say, "It's marital's fault," yet how convenient it is to blame "marital" for it. Marriages could be healed, improved, and moved to real intimacy if the same energy it takes to maintain and defend the labels was used to own up to our behavior, confess our role in the breakdowns, and offer some hope and commitment that things will change.

Take responsibility for your part in relationships today, married or not.

- *Do I own any labels to negate my responsibility or avoid accountability?*
- *Have I put labels on my spouse in the form of judgments and pessimism?*

Self-control is nothing more than managing life from the inside out.

Self-control is like weight training. Exercise it and gain some emotional muscle.

Whether you believe in the Bible or not, there's a verse that suggests, "It's not what goes into a person that defiles them, but what comes out of them." One aspect of what goes into a person is that during life, we will take in our fair share of deception, verbal assaults, and betrayals—meaning we will intake a variety of letdowns, and they will come from friends, family, co-workers, and strangers. But when these letdowns show up, we'll have one of two options: maintain our emotions and govern life the way we want, *or* give our life to someone else to control how we feel, influence our state of mind, and govern our existence for a time. It's an important choice to make, because as we get older and become less tolerant of these things, others inflicting their own brand of stress and breakdown on our lives will not only increase, it will compound. So if you'd like to reduce the repercussions and gain strength in this area, the first step is to hold every person or situation that upsets you as a provision to practice self-control . . . key word being *practice*, because nobody owns self-control and it's not a trait we typically master, nor do we aspire to. But as we exercise self-control, we will begin to see that its long-term value far outweighs the desire to remove control out of our actions for a brief moment. So rather than burn bridges, you become better at building them. Instead of inducing stress into situations, you usher in a calm, a hope, and a maturity that rubs off positively on the offending parties. Practice will never make perfect here, but perfect isn't the measure. More peace, prosperity, and potential for progress are the measure.

Get control of self-control so you stay in control today.

- *Do I welcome problems as opportunities to improve my self-control?*
- *What would life be like if I focused intently on governing my emotions?*

Sometimes in order for things to be better, things have to be in better order.

The value in becoming organized is that life suddenly becomes more harmonized.

I've heard it said that we should either move or burn our house down every seven years just to get rid of the stuff we accumulate. Well, stuff creates clutter, clutter creates disarray, disarray creates anxiety, and anxiety creates loss of productivity and enthusiasm. So the basics of getting organized start with the removal of things we don't need, want, or use anymore. There are plenty of charities that will benefit from your purging, and you'll also feel lighter emotionally when it's done. More advanced organization starts with making sure that everything you own has a place and the proximity of those things is well thought out. Tools in one spot, business things in another, crafts and hobbies in another. Make sure everything is accessible and easy to find.

Then there are the things we use on a day-to-day basis. For example, my car keys and wallet go in the same place every time now, because I would waste countless hours every year trying to find out where I put them, and my wife would be taken out of *her* productivity because of my idiocy. Shame on *me* for not fixing it sooner. The goal here is to identify the areas of stress or unproductivity with the things we own or have to do, and to develop a system, process, or place for everything. It's either that or we allocate time to *managing chaos* instead of *making progress*. Not to mention, the amount of time it takes to get organized is fractional in contrast to the time it takes to deal with disarray. And once you're about 15 percent into the process of organizing, you'll begin to see what it means when your things, responsibilities, and life are in order.

To minimize unnecessary strife, organize your life today.

- *How often do I search for things because they don't have a designated place?*
- *Would I have more time for important things if my life were better organized?*

For those who can't see the light at the end of the tunnel, the tunnel may be curved. Therefore the light is at the end of the curve—the learning curve.

If life came with a manual, it would be forty miles thick and would take several lifetimes to get through. It would also be pretty useless, considering that our life is different from the next person's and so on. However, it seems the older I get, the more things confront me where I have no previous experience or frame of reference. As a result, the first feeling I get when something new pops up is a feeling of uncertainty, and in some cases it goes as far as inadequacy. And yet I'm not supposed to know what to do, because it is new. The fact remains that nearly all of the stress we experience today has to do with things that are unknown to us. Whether career, relationships, health, or otherwise . . . our perspective is always clouded and our confidence always flimsy when we know little about the issue, the subject, the situation, the person, and in some cases, even the opportunity. But whatever exists or comes into our life that we're uncertain of can always be tamed if we immediately begin a journey of learning instead of wondering or over-thinking. First responders in the medical profession are trained to do the same drill every time a catastrophe hits. Our discipline to handle new circumstances should be similar. We should move into the mode of discovery and use every means necessary to get schooled up on what is real, how we can deal, and then see how we feel. The truth is that our levels of confidence and clarity will generally be proportionate to the depth of our inquiry.

Don't let unfamiliar circumstances alarm you; let them teach you today.

- *What one area of my life would benefit from an infusion of learning?*
- *Do I need to improve my online search skills or increase advisory resources?*

If you speak and others don't hear, it's not that they didn't listen, it's that you failed to resonate.

As a conservative count, I can say there are at least ten thousand times in my life (and counting) when I blamed someone for not listening to what I said, only to have them come back and tell me they heard it differently or didn't hear it at all. It has caused more relational grief, hindered my career, and stifled my progress more than any other area. But I still struggle with the reality that I am quick to conclude they didn't listen, they're out to lunch, or they're just an idiot. For most of my adult life, it never crossed my mind that it might be what I said, didn't say, or more importantly how I said what I said that created the roadblock to effective communication. It never dawned on me that because people are different and need to be communicated to in different ways that I might be the one with the communication problem (the idiot), and guess what—*I was.*

With a renewed commitment to specificity, sensitivity, and slowing down, every delegation, negotiation, and conversation became more effective when I took a moment to reflect on how the other would best receive what I was saying, or how much or little to say and how best to deliver it. When I began to communicate in details and write things down for others, chances of my communication being heard and agendas being accomplished were generally twice as good.

Communicate with resonance and specificity today.

- *What are my communication breakdowns? Am I a detailed communicator?*
- *What areas are in need of writing things down or speaking in greater detail?*

Move at the pace of appreciation.

Life is a pace, not a race. It's more about having moments than chasing momentum.

Someone once said, the problem with life in the fast lane is you get to the end too quickly. And that is a fact! Life moves at such a speed that if we get caught up in it, we'll have years feeling like months and hours like minutes, especially as we get older. The good news is how we hold time can have the opposite effect. We can extend life by increasing the value of moments, and if we move at a pace by which we take in instead of blast by, our time will count for more, thereby enriching life, and in some strange way . . . extending it.

Being a fast-lane guy myself, I am blessed that my wife helps me keep perspective. She once said to me, "Honey, you need to move at the pace of appreciation." Her quote, not mine. "What do you mean?" I said, hurrying to get through the conversation. She replied, "I just believe that you miss so much of what's in front of your eyes by focusing beyond into what is not yet here." She hit a bull's-eye right between the ears. So in that moment, I forced myself to slow down—way down—to see what was in front of me, and it was my amazing wife. Not only did she look different to me at the pace of appreciation, but I saw a beauty, both inside and out, that I'd been rushing by all too often. For the moment, I saw past my busyness and was at total peace downshifting into a gear where I could see clearly, which inherently *is* the pace of appreciation. It's a slower place than we're used to, but the value and beauty that reside there make it worth the investment.

Move at the pace of appreciation today.

- *Where do I tend to move too fast and miss the value of what's in front of me?*
- *How much more would I appreciate if I moved at the pace of appreciation?*

Do we see people for who they are now or who they are becoming?

I'm sure if I were to ask about your growth in life, you'd say you were a notably different person today than you were X years ago, maybe even X months ago. That's because people are dynamic and live in a constant state of transformation of character. Aside from rare cases, we generally get better with age—wiser and more generous.

So why is it we look at others and judge them if we see things in their current way of being that go against our grain? Why do we place our biases, labels, and hypotheses on people based on who they are today, rather than forgo our assumptions and pessimism and see them for who they are becoming—and maybe even help them along?

The main reason is that it's easier to dismiss people than to invest in them. When we only see people for who they are today (especially when we don't like what we see), our attitude toward them exudes skepticism and indifference, all because we are stuck in the reality of what is now and not the possibility of what is to come. This posture not only creates relational dysfunction and breakdown, it's a self-centered and self-righteous stance that offers nothing to others, as well as nothing to ourselves. In contrast, when we see people in light of who they are becoming, they will know that we are on their side, that we see possibility in them. The tangible effects of such support create rapport and trust that are rarely surpassed by other more traditional forms of encouragement.

If you want to know the best time to see greatness in people today, look at your watch!

- *Do I see people for who they are and merely stop at that?*
- *What would my relationships be like if I looked for who they are becoming?*

For those who think that they're getting away with it, think again!

It's amazing how well we hide things in plain sight! In life, we develop our little secret things we desire to keep hidden from others. I won't list what they are, as there are many, but *you know* what they are. You've either had, have, or will have things in your life, where you say to yourself, "Cool, nobody knows I'm doing this. I'm just going to keep going until I get caught." Too late! (I'll explain in a minute.) The illusion that we're hiding things from others presupposes that if others in our life don't know the exact nature of the things we are doing in secret, then there's no harm in doing what we're doing. There's a problem with that. If you are doing something that someone doesn't know about, they will with absolute certainty know that *something* is going on, and they will begin to invent assumptions about what might be amiss. And although their assumptions may not be accurate, they still get to experience the fullness of what it is you're doing in secret in the ways it affects how you engage in the relationship or don't. The sad part here is that the other person experiences the repercussions of the hidden activities without being able to put a finger on it, so they get the added bonus of thinking it might be them that is causing what's missing in the relationship. This could be the closest thing to adding insult to injury that I've seen. So what is hidden is not really hidden at all; it's just *not* labeled and perhaps *not* dealt with. In the long run, these things *do* get exposed, and the damage that's done through them when caught is nothing compared to all the weeks, months, and years of keeping it hidden in plain sight.

Consider that the victim of hidden behaviors isn't others; it's the one doing the hiding who is the victim.

- *How are the things you keep hidden affecting your relationships?*
- *Are those around you blaming themselves because you're unwilling to confess?*

Does attitude motivate us to work or does work motivate our attitude?

I was going to start a pessimists' club, but I didn't think it would work. Then I was going to start an optimists' club, but I felt it was too good to be true. This proves it's not always the attitude that gets the work done . . . it's the *work* that gets the work done.

Napoleon hated himself. He loathed the way he looked and struggled with self-esteem and yet accomplished much in his lifetime. In short (no pun intended), he was considered one of the greatest military commanders of all time. Countless individuals who have made notable differences in the world did so by moving ahead with their vision for their life. By ignoring liability-riddled attitudes, they stepped into their destiny somewhat blind, but with enough foresight to know what was on the other side of a commitment that disregarded feelings and ignored the idea that starting a vision required the perfect attitude.

The proof is in—self-esteem or the right attitude is not needed to execute on a vision; it's just an asset to it. As one who has high regard for our thought life, it pains me to say that attitude is overrated; but when it comes to work . . . it is. If I had a dollar for every time someone told me that "how they felt" was the reason they didn't get busy and get things done, I'd be rich. There's a trap we must be aware of that the attitudes that would drive us to success should appear out of nowhere prior to starting the work. Lost in *that* paradigm, we abandon the reality that a healthy attitude might just come after we start moving. There's a concept! I've always believed that the lasting motivation to do anything comes 5 to 10 percent into the process, and rarely before, which makes starting something that much more appealing, not to mention . . . more attainable.

Start that one thing you haven't "felt" like starting today.

- *Am I waiting for the right attitude before I start something?*
- *What one project could I just start on and see if the attitude follows?*

If you have the courage to admit it when you're wrong, you'll be right 100 percent of the time.

There are few things more right in life than admitting when we are wrong.

If you're leading a somewhat normal life, chances are you've been wrong a few times and will probably be wrong a few more before you clock out. Now consider that if you desire to go beyond a normal life and accomplish extraordinary things, you can multiply your upcoming wrongs to the tune of ridiculous. Although risk equals more wrongs, there is inherent beauty in being wrong as long as you are not caught up in the illusion that being wrong—just isn't right. The beauty comes in admitting to others and ourselves when we've erred. In fact, three of the most powerful words in our language are "I was wrong." There's a humility in those words that will have us stare "wrongdoings" in the face, saying, "Yeah, so what if I got it wrong? I'm learning, growing, and further along for taking a chance. What else you got?"

Although it's difficult to admit when we've erred, the need to never be wrong is a disease that destroys relationships and will taint any harmony we have with ourselves. Not to confuse the desire to be right with the need to be right. The desire to be accurate, to deliver excellence, and to succeed is wisdom. The unwavering need to always be right ensures a life of performance anxiety, insecurity, even loneliness. People don't mind being around those who confess wrongdoings but will go out of their way to avoid those needing to be perfect. There is great liberty knowing you can freely admit your breakdowns to anyone at any time. People respect it and learn from it, and you learn too!

Admit it if you happen to be wrong today.

- *Do I admit when I'm wrong, or is my instinct to cover up or manipulate?*
- *Will others be disappointed or refreshed if I admit when I'm wrong?*

Everything in life is about selling: Either you'll influence them, or they'll influence you.

Everything you look at, sit on, drive, eat, play with, and experience is here because someone persuaded someone else that it should be here. Persuasion is the key to every innovation; even persuading ourselves that we can innovate and make it happen is a serious battle. Add to the mix that others may be trying to convince us things can't be done, and World War III is here . . . the war of persuasions. Win, lose, or draw, life is about selling someone on who, what, when, where, why, and how it should or could be. Whether from clients, prospects, spouses, friends, kids, or even strangers, we live in a constant competition of persuasions, and as much as we'd like it to be a little less competitive and a little more based on the merits of our ideas, it's just not so.

If you want to move agendas and get things done, it's best to embrace the necessity of persuasion, even if you have to change the word *sell* to *convince, move, influence,* or whatever fits your style. Even a subtle change in terms can make us more at ease with the inevitable path of persuasion.

Here's what makes the concept palatable: Selling is serving, and we'd be well served to sell ourselves on that idea. In its purest, most honest form, selling is nothing more than paving the way to create value for others and providing something that will improve their circumstances. It's a noble cause, and we should never feel guilty or intrusive for sharing something that moves others to a beneficial action or result. So call the process what you like, do it the way it feels right to you, but persuade away. The world will be a better, livelier place because of it.

Work on your own style of persuasion today!

- *Do I view persuasion as selling or serving?*
- *What in my life is sitting on the sidelines, underdeveloped or undersold?*

The most crippling of all conditions is not a disease, a syndrome, or a disorder but a mind plagued with negative thoughts.

In life, it's never "what it is" that matters, but how you hold it that counts.

In my lifetime, I've met people who have physical issues from insignificant to almost unfathomable, and yet they maintain an extraordinary view on life, others, and their circumstances. Despite what may have occurred at birth, along the way, or in thinking of what's ahead, they not only have enough fuel in their perspective to drive a healthy personal lifestyle, they have enough in reserve to be an inspiration to others. And if you ask any one of them about the foundation for their view on life, you'll hear a common denominator: "There was a point where I chose to have a perspective that would work, not one of what was. And once the choice was made, I began to live out my life in alignment with that decision."

Let's face it, there are few things in life we can change in a second or two, but one change we can make immediately is how we think. And like our muscles, the more you exercise your mind, the more it works for you. You have to begin the process of exercising it to max out what is possible from it. Modern psychology calls it reframing; the Bible calls it renewing of the mind. Regardless, the process of creating perspectives that work is not only attainable, it's predictable if you put the time in. I guess if everyday living can be summed up in a phrase, it might be, "Circumstances: It's not what they are but how we relate to them that matters." Mental fitness requires that we remain conscious of how we're relating to life and to others, and a little "perspective exercise" can go a long way here.

It's even better to be negatively positive than positively negative today.

- *Is my overall perspective on life one of optimism, pessimism, or neutrality?*
- *What specific areas of my life could use a perspective tune-up?*

Pretentiousness is a *fool*-time job!

Have you ever taken the time to evaluate your authenticity around other people? In the earlier years of my life, I was lonely, emotionally inept, and as ego-driven as they come. Regardless of the circumstance, I always felt the need for validation and would sheepishly become whatever made the best impression for the situation or group of people I was with. Keeping up my image was a full-time job, until one day I realized that the energy I was using to protect my image and create façades (big or small) could be used to create more value in the lives of others, and I'd also have more energy and focus to do many other great things. Life took on a whole new meaning when I dropped the façades and just became me.

But even though we may have a handle on our image, we all live with façades from time to time. For some it's often; for others who are blessed to be at peace with who they are, it's rare, but it does creep in. To compound the issue, there are the different circles of life we travel in, such as home, business, social circles, affinity groups, the gym, activity clubs, and many more. Façades can show up at different levels of intensity in different areas of our life, and wearing our masks for too long is enough to drive anyone back to simply being real.

Although deciding to be fully yourself, authentic, and transparent is a little scary at first, there is real terror in thinking you could live your life where no one around you would know the real you . . . including you. The adjustment of "just being you," consistently and without reservation, is a magnificent journey of truth that will reveal your good traits and your bad traits. The good you get to flow with; the bad you get to work on. Either way, the true *you* becomes more grounded, more aware, and more at peace in life with every authentic moment.

**Drop the agenda of impressing others
today and just BE!**

- *In what area does my need to impress others become a source
  of anxiety?*
- *Have I spent time contemplating who I have committed
  to be in life?*

Sometimes we think the only common ground we have with someone is the ground we are both standing on.

Few beliefs are more tragic than "We have nothing in common." It may seem the odds of finding common ground with certain people are similar to lottery odds, and they can be if we aspire to mediocrity rather than possibility. The belief that there are certain people whom we'll never have synergy with is simply an indication of social resignation or is a sign that our relationship skills have become sedated. For those interested in becoming relationally confident, more effective—even brilliant—it's wise to embrace the idea that finding common ground with others can be an enjoyable activity. "But people are different," we say. Yes, people are different, sometimes appear boring, or seem like they're from another planet, but it's wise to realize that *every* conversation is a possibility, not a limitation, and is a clear opportunity to discover common ground and improve relational acumen. All people are interesting in direct proportion to our commitment to inquire into their life and draw things out of them. In every person, there are experiences, expertise, stories, and textures that are unique to them and will be common to us.

The question becomes—will I take the time to discover what is there, or will I count it another unfounded judgment or a quick bout of social laziness to discover the beauty of commonality? The truth is people are never boring; our untuned skills to find common ground are boring and limiting.

Find common ground with someone you may not have it with today.

- *Has ignoring common ground limited my personal and business relationships?*
- *Who do I feel I have no common ground with? Who can I practice on?*

Derivations of the truth
will bring exasperation to the soul.

Liar, liar, life's on fire.

The statement "To lie or not to lie" appears to take on a different meaning when you say, "To exaggerate or not to exaggerate." The truth is, they're one and the same, but exaggerating is a bit easier on our conscience. So why do we feel the need to manipulate the truth from ever so slightly to the extreme?

The answer is fear. We simply become afraid that the truth won't do its job, it will fall short in some way, and we might wind up a fool. So we resort to a lie, and when the lie spins into a web of confusion and breakdown, the need to pile lie on top of lie becomes apparent until the truth finds its way out. By then, the state of the relationship we've been lying to resembles a train wreck, and cleaning up the mess requires some heavy lifting. It would be wise to have more fear of lying than of sharing things exactly the way they are.

Whether half-truths, partial truths, or little white lies, we can package our "honesty" not so honestly. Consider at times that we can be just as artful in delivering "strategic truths" as we can be in delivering flat-out deception, and again consider they're one and the same.

In contrast, there is great peace to be had in life simply by sharing things exactly the way they are, freeing our mind to think of more productive things, and not having to remember the myriad of slight exaggerations that will ultimately come back to bite us in an exaggerated fashion.

Lose the temptation to manipulate your truth today.

- *Where do I feel tempted to stretch the truth in my life?*
- *Am I done with the crazy notion that lying is safer than the truth?*

Each day is better dealt with within the confines of itself.

The deal of the day is to always deal *in* the day.

People who live a discontented life filled with more downs than ups are usually suffering from a mental warehouse overflowing with a buildup of things that have not been dealt with. A rarely talked about reality is that a life of discontentment is seldom the outcome of a single large event. It is generally the result of daily issues that are left unresolved, causing them to spill over to the next day, onto our mind-set, and into our attitude. After enough time passes by, they compound into an insurmountable burden that spurs restlessness, anxiety, and stress. The "deal with the excessive load once in a while" strategy may work occasionally, but while we live in postponement and avoidance of daily dealing, we carry an unnecessary burden, resulting in poor overall life performance—a heavy emotional load that drags us down, even pulls us backward. The real danger if we avoid issues for too long is that they become more difficult to recognize, making them harder to work with. Add the fact that we're busy contending with the most recent batch of unresolved matters, and it becomes a big pile of horrible.

In contrast to avoidance, the habit of dealing with what comes up in a day within the confines of the day gives us opportunities to deal in smaller, more focused bits that aren't mixed into the confusion of other undone stuff. The confidence and skills we gain through this discipline can make whatever comes up in the day have us saying "No big deal" rather than "I just can't deal" with consistency and leverage.

Deal with something that is undone today for a more productive and peaceful tomorrow.

- *What undone stuff needs to be handled once and for all?*
- *How much lighter would I feel if I didn't let my issues build up?*

"Monetary lessons" are better as eye-openers than wallet openers.

There are seasons, even years of life, where financial resources are thin, and there can be times when money flows like the rapids. Today, money is moving like molasses in the freezer rather than flowing, and I have a feeling it's going to be this way for some time and perhaps get worse. This is to say whatever it is we currently have is precious and some of what we take in should make its way into the storehouse. We all know mistakes can be costly on multiple fronts. They can take away energy, time, focus, and resources, all of which translate in some way to a financial burden.

But through something known as the six degrees of separation, there is comfort in knowing that we have direct or indirect access to people who can help us avoid these expensive learning lessons before they open our wallet. Through leveraging our relationships, we *all* have access to world-class knowledge in just about every category of life. It's the "I know someone who knows someone or might know someone" reality that ensures we have access to answers. It just takes a little digging. For the most part, valuable advice is just one to three phone calls away, and the truth is . . . those who are learned in the areas we need help with are generally willing to share what they know with us. More often than not, they are passionate about it and love to talk about it. Unfortunately, complacency and pride can get in the way of getting the insights we need. A little work and humility in the asking pale in comparison to the price we pay to remain ignorant of the things we could easily learn.

Identify a challenge and source out some wisdom today.

- Who are my resources for learning, and who do I know that is well connected?
- What one thing in my life should I move toward getting some perspective on?

It's not your clothes but who you are in them that makes you fashionable.

The way to be most fashionable is to dress to be uniquely you.

Movie stars and other famous people have an uncanny ability to set trends that the human race follows to the thread, the color, and the style, whether the trend is aesthetically pleasing or not. These aggressive looks can be reflective of a celebrity's midlife crisis, a recent divorce and need of a new look, aging and looking for that youthful spin, or just a whim to be cool—things that have little to do with us. But the next thing you know, there's a rush to go buy clothing that through some magical lens is going to make others look upon us with starstruck eyes. Ain't gonna happen, not in this lifetime or any other. Fact is, it's quite laughable when you see look-alike attempts that for obvious reasons fall short of the intended goal. It might be wise the next time a new trend hits to repeat a dozen times, "I'm just not Brad Pitt," or "I'm just not Angelina Jolie."

You've heard it said that how we dress says a lot about *who* we are. That's true, but it's only a fraction of it. The bulk of it depends on who we are being and how we feel while in the clothes we're wearing. Our character, our personality, and our capacity to love, encourage, and be a blessing to others has nothing to do with DKNY, Armani, or St. John, and everything to do with our inner beauty. I'm sure we'd rather be comfortable with who we are as a person than what we're wearing any day of the week. And at the rate fashion trends change and celebrities switch looks, it's economically beneficial as well.

Be fashionable from the inside out today.

- *Have I considered what it might look like to dress "extraordinarily me"?*
- *Have I considered the attractiveness of what's inside as well?*

Sometimes the best counsel we can give someone is delivered in the form of a question.

Well-thought-out questions are often more powerful than well-thought-out statements. Safer too.

Most of our communication efforts are spent discovering ways to say things more clearly, accurately, and powerfully. But little thought goes into the concept of becoming an expert at asking questions as a tool to help people instead of making the statements we think are so poignant. Questions are the assurance of intelligent, impactful communication, and the more the questions, the less chance of a miscommunication.

The art of uncovering what is real for people is a lost art, as it takes patience to listen through the stories, the pain, and whatever else has to come out before the raw truth surfaces. But the value that exists in strategic inquiry is far greater in effectiveness than taking potshots at someone's issues without knowing the background and the facts. It is in the exposure of these details that effective dialogue will begin to form, creating wise, accurate statements that hit home, rather than broad strokes that have little meaning and potentially no impact.

I remember talking with a psychologist friend over lunch, and I asked, "Wouldn't it be amazing if during a patient session you didn't make one statement, but simply asked all the right questions? Then after the patient answered all your questions, they got it and were on the path to recovery?" He laughed, then replied, "The skill of questioning is the top skill for anyone looking to have impact with others." Providing someone with the space to discover and voice their own revelations is wisdom at its finest. Our ability to "strategically inquire" is a learned skill that will pay a lifetime of emotional, relational, and financial dividends, and if you ask me, it's well worth the effort.

Try asking questions rather than making statements today.

- *Am I inclined to one-way broadcast or intelligent inquiry?*
- *What would conversations look like if I became a master of questions?*

Breathe your way into a peaceful state.

If breathing is sustenance to life, why can't it be used to improve it? Take a look around. Do you see people in a state of constant joy and relative contentment, or are there looks of trepidation, concern, and just keeping things under control? If you look closely and long enough, you'll find people are in a state of constant contemplation about how to achieve more peace, joy, and ways to thrive in life, with peace being foundational.

Aside from spiritual paradigms about peace, which I am convinced are the only lasting way to sustain peace, there are several things we can do to enter into a more relaxed state. The most overlooked and effective stress reduction remedy is instantly accessible, doesn't require a prescription, and last I checked, it's free—*breathing*.

Most people function in "shallow breathing mode," an unhealthy mode driven by the pace of life, not the pace of healthy breathing. Over time, the body adopts the habit of shallow breathing mode, and then it doesn't receive enough oxygen to do what the body is supposed to do—regulate, revitalize, and invigorate cells. Breathing exercises are nothing short of a miracle for the body. They allow us a new form of control and a way to deal with stress that is completely natural and almost supernatural at the same time. Knowing the ramifications of not breathing for five minutes, we should have no reason to underestimate deep and controlled breathing as a viable tool to reduce stress and impact the body in a positive way. Type in "breathing exercises" online, and you'll come up with enough breathing lessons to give you a mild case of stress. My suggestion? Go to one of the sites, give breathing a try, and get rid of that stress.

Learn about how therapeutic breathing can help you today.

- *Have I taken notice of how I breathe in everyday life?*
- *What times of the day would make sense to start a deep-breathing regimen?*

It may be wrong to put the cart before the horse, but it's never wrong to put the heart before the course.

Life direction. It's not always so obvious, is it? There are many considerations, including basic necessities, peer pressure, what am I good at, will it work, am I certain, and a few hundred other variables that either set us in the wrong direction or have us stuck in a rut so deep that no one above can hear us shout. At the core of all these questions is the one thing we know to be true, and that is our hearts—the true feelings we have when we ignore all the noise of life, the opinions of the skeptics, and the implied rules that have the ability to govern us into misery.

Case in point: A friend became an attorney in part because many of his family members were attorneys. More and more he struggles to accept that his passion, heart, and character don't align with his current area of practice. Today, he is coming to terms with the reality that his heart is not in this course and there may be greater satisfaction found in doing what he loves.

The value in doing what we love is manifold: We usually do it better, we always strive to improve, we rarely get burned out, and we generally rise to the top. And those who do what they are passionate about sleep better and wake up differently than those caught in the drudge; they define themselves as rich, regardless of how much money, accolades, and notoriety they attain. I've not known many who have allowed their passion to choose their profession to have regrets. But I have seen many who chose their profession for ulterior motives that came from the mind and not the heart experience great conflict and compromise.

**Time is ticking.
Isn't it time to start doing what you love today?**

- *Is what I'm doing a one-way, dead-end street to my happiness?*
- *What possibilities exist in moving into what I love in the next one, three, or five years?*

Love is not so much revealed in how we feel about others but in how we deal with others.

*L*ove. It's one of those words that gets confused in the mix of feelings, relational dynamics, psychological terminology, and more. And yet it is the most powerful driving force on the planet—one that people live for and are willing to die for. The word *love* has more definitions, implications, and confusions than most any other word in the English language. For example, the average dictionary is more like a "fictionary" when it says that love is "a feeling of warm personal attachment or deep affection." Actually, these are the outcomes of love and not love itself, as love is not a thing, it's an action—not a noun, but a verb. In fact, a high percentage of definitions and how we view love are based around how a person *feels* rather than how they *act*. Perhaps that's why we see the world as more feeling-driven than commitment-driven.

Perhaps you've heard the reference that we are to love our neighbors as we love ourselves (neighbors meaning the ones geographically closest to us at any one moment in time). The love spoken of here isn't a feeling but rather a call to serve others whether it feels right or not. The levels of warmth, attachment, and affection that we often mistake for love are generally proportional to how committed we are to loving unconditionally and with ongoing sacrifice. When we place the needs of others above our own, this is the beginning of love and the richness and feelings that come with it.

Show real love today, even if you have to sacrifice to do so!

- *Do I view love as a feeling or as an action that creates feelings of love?*
- *What sacrifices could I make that would show love to those I say I care about?*

The moment I focused on saying less, I began to communicate more.

Never underestimate the gift of brevity.

From the beginning of time until 2005, a certain amount of information was disseminated into society. Today, that same amount of information is delivered into society every forty-eight hours. Every day a million new websites are launched, millions of blogs are expanded, and thousands of books are published. Words, words, and more words, many of them a waste of paper and pixels. And some of them are mine. Guilty. As a writer for various business publications, I was often criticized for verbosity, even though the content was well received. So one of the reasons I started writing *ShiftPoints* was to challenge myself to communicate more effectively with fewer words. And one of the reasons I named my branding agency Breviti was to provide concise branding and positioning to my clients, so they could break through the clutter of marketing that said so much it said *nothing* because no one actually read it.

Since writing *ShiftPoints* and launching Breviti, I've been working to bring my communication and writing to a new level of brevity and clarity. I'm more selective about the words I use, I think more before I speak or write, and I'm more aware of others' time and attention span . . . lucky for them. There is great value to be had in the practice of saying less and meaning more. It's a challenge and a game that increases our effectiveness, improves our energy level, and makes us more beneficial to those in our personal and business lives. It also creates more time to listen.

Challenge yourself to say more with less today!

- *Am I conscious of the words I use, or do I have Autopilot Mouth Syndrome?*
- *Would I be so bold to ask others if I talk too much or write too long?*

My commitment is to be late once more in my life—when I stop breathing and become the late Dean Del Sesto.

I'm not sure about you, but there are few things that bother me more than someone being late. As a result, I make every effort to be early to meetings by at least five minutes, because I believe it to be impossible to be on time. Think about it. Every watch is different, so to be on time would require that all have the same standard of time, which means we'd all be sporting an atomic clock. And we'd have to arrive at the exact second to be on time. Highly unlikely.

So that means we're either early or late. And the time frame that reflects well on our character and our outcomes is to be early and well prepared, every time, without fail. I come from the school that if I'm late to a meeting without notification in advance, it is a direct reflection of how much I care for the people I am meeting with. And if I'm consistently late but use notification as a strategy to be late all the time, I would still have to look at how much I care about those I'm always late for. Lateness shows lack of respect, and it is a leader in creating frustration and anxiety in others. Since I realized my personal brand would take a hit and I'd lose credibility with others, my "early" percentage is 95 percent, and as for the other 5 percent, I call as far in advance as I can because *my life* isn't the only one that matters. We all know there are meetings we'll never be late for and ones that rank low on the "get there on time" scale. But if we truly embraced the idea that our reputation, character, and influence were declining each time we were late, we'd design our lives for timeliness, not flakiness.

How much you care shows up in the details, so be on time today.

- *When am I consistently late, and why am I late with some and not others?*
- *What things do I need to adjust in my life so I can be early . . . every time?*

If you want to be a giver, take the following to heart!

If we all understood the value in giving over taking and how little it takes to give, we wouldn't always give in to feeling taken or needing to take. So always take the opportunity to give, and you'll have something worth taking, give or take a little.

There are givers in life and there are takers. We generally love to be around givers. We go out of our way to help them, they always have our ear, and we'll usually be there for them regardless of their need or want. As for takers, we don't like to be around them, and we question how much pain there will be while engaged with them. We are keenly aware that they are the kind of people who can improve a gathering by leaving it, and we'll do what we can to assist in that process. And yet most takers will not admit they are takers; they won't even *give* it a consideration. Although there is constant conflict and relational breakdown in their lives, most takers are not willing to look closely at the results of their relationships and often blame others for any breakdowns. This is the one case where taking would do them some good—in the form of taking ownership.

When I counsel people on relationships, my first order of business is to discover whether they're in the habit of giving more or taking more. If they're having relationship issues, "taking" is usually the winner about, oh . . . 100 percent of the time. My next step, and this is key, is to help them discover the unmet needs of those they're in relationship with and switch them into giving mode to meet those unmet needs. The results? I don't counsel for very long, because giving ultimately meets everyone's needs, including the need we all have to live out our lives, not over-process them.

Give more and take less today!

- *Am I more of a giver or a taker?*
- *If I am a taker with certain people, what could being a giver bring to life?*

Winners don't dwell on "what's wrong." They work on "what's next."

Problems are like disease. The faster they're dealt with . . . the better. Although there is value to be had when a problem arises in our life, problems are not our friends, so we are not supposed to hang out with them for extended periods of time. The goal is to treat them with urgent care, not as a disease that requires long-term care. I call the disease *Problem-itis*, the condition of allowing a problem to hinder or paralyze clear thinking to get past the problem. *Disease* is a strong word, I know. But problems can become a disease if we entertain them for a while, and the "avoidance of dealing" becomes a habit.

We all know life is riddled with obstacles and a diverse array of chaos. You are in the midst of some of those things now, or there's some waiting around the corner. So imagine the habit of encountering problems where your first instinct and immediate reaction are to work problems out, not invite them in. It's not about pushing the problem away as much as it is bringing it in close enough to scrutinize it, see the full repercussions of its impact, and work it through.

Consider that having a consistent process for problem solving can make the next problem that hits you feel more like a feather than a hammer. Part of that process is having trusted others to talk with and access to information to dig into. (Type just about any problem into Google, and you'll find no shortage of potential solutions, and as a bonus, you'll find out you're not alone in whatever the issue is.)

Got a problem?
Work on what's next more than what's wrong.

• *Am I more inclined to focus on what's wrong or on what's next?*
• *What one problem keeps coming back that I haven't dealt with?*

The outcome of your presentation is heavily influenced by the conviction you bring into the room.

If you're ever at a gathering and you take a moment to people watch, you'll notice that whoever is leading the meeting enters the room with a noticeable presence. You'll either see things like tentativeness, reluctance, frustration, anxiety, or arrogance, or you'll see enthusiasm, preparedness, calmness, confidence, and conviction. Regardless, we generally start to feel the same things we see—it's almost a mirror. When a presenter walks into a room and the intent of their heart is to serve, we feel served; when they show up to respect our time, we feel respected; and when they arrive with humility, we feel relaxed and ready to receive what they have to say. I'm not sure about you, but I've had it with perfectly polished presentations, disconnected regurgitation, and presentations devoid of heart.

In a world of too many words and too much content, people aren't moved so much by the words we say as by who we're being and how convicted we are with our words. Audiences are moved and persuaded to listen by a presenter's commitment to them rather than some form of showmanship. The value can never be found in our content or delivery alone; the value reveals itself in our authenticity, conviction, and how much we genuinely want those in the room to benefit from what we have to say. These are the things that shift paradigms, make people come alive, and move them to life-changing action.

Ultimately, it's the conviction we carry and the concern for the growth of our audience that will convey our verbal and nonverbal communication. Anything else is a waste of time, oxygen, and in some cases—money.

**Make sure your presence is a present
to all who are in the room.**

- *Do I bring a caring, passionate heart to meetings or just a bunch of data?*
- *When presenting, will I spend time to consider what I've committed to cause in my listeners?*

Are you sitting back "waiting to be discovered" or going out to "discover what's waiting"?

Many a grave is filled with talent that never lived.

Throughout history, there are simply too many people above and below ground who never fulfilled their dreams because of the buzz-phrase "waiting to be discovered." It's not a phrase we say out loud or even read about that often, if ever. It's the kind of phrase that lives in our thoughts and fantasies. It keeps progress on hold, and with each day that goes by it makes our talents rustier, more distant, and less alive. But hey, you have talent, I have talent, we've all got talent, but here are two critical words that should bring a bit of reality to our talent set: "So what!"

On the one hand, talent is a springboard for success and fulfillment. On the other, it can be a liability if we think that talent by itself will walk through doors that need to be pushed, kicked open, or broken down in order to gain traction. The other liability of talent is when we get too caught up in our gifts and adopt the attitude of, "I'm entitled, I've paid my dues, I'll be discovered, my talent will make way for itself."

Well, here are two more applicable words—"lottery odds." The days of "opportunity knocks" are quickly becoming past tense, and the idea of people having pockets of time to go out and discover talent may have been fine when the population was half the current size and world conditions were a bit more relaxed. But in the new global economy and connectivity, competition is fierce, and talent being equal, progress starts when you discover unique ways to get your gifting in front of new people with new ways to create more value. The next step, whether online or off-line, is to tell that story, the difference and the value you bring to as many people as you can, daily, hourly . . . perpetually, but never stop!

Get your talent in front of others today!

- *What percentage of effort am I exercising to get my talents in front of others?*
- *The clock is ticking. How much time do I have left? Is the window closing?*

People are literally a canvas we can paint with our behavior.

Whoever said you can't change a person is the person who could stand a change.

Ever notice that what comes from people during our interactions with them is largely linked to what we draw out of them—good or bad? It may not be that we change them permanently, but for that exchange, interaction, or conversation, we have the capacity to bring out both beauty in people and things that are not so beautiful. I know I've hurt those who are close to me in horrific ways. And if I take a moment to recount those events and the hurt I caused, I can see their faces and their hurt as if it were yesterday. I should know. I painted on their canvas with either my betrayal, my hurtful words, or my harmful actions. Not that I'm a total lost cause, as I've learned from those experiences. Through that learning, I've also painted some pretty good pictures, and today I am committed to using the art of me to paint more *good* interactions and memories than *bad*.

It's no great revelation that the interactions we have with others are cause and effect, but it's commonplace to emotionally disconnect from what we're causing or not causing during exchanges. The mindset becomes resigned to thinking, "People just are what they are," rather than proclaiming, "People can be what I draw out of them," or in this metaphor . . . "paint into them with my actions." We all want the best from others but often underestimate our capacity to bring it out.

Consider that people are simply . . . who you are for them. Through our own art-form, we can facilitate people's anger into happiness, sadness into laughter, complacency into action, and cynicism into optimism. Of course, it's not our *responsibility* to do so, it's just our *opportunity*. There's no shortage of need and an endless supply of paint. Your paint.

Paint value onto the canvas of others' lives today!

- *Have I considered the way I engage with people as a creative endeavor?*
- *Are my social paintings abstract, surreal, paint splats, beautiful, or childlike?*

The control of health care costs begins with self-control.

We don't have a health care problem in this world as much as a "care for our health" problem. Our life depends on good health, but our health depends on us. From physical to psychological problems or combinations of both, there is great opportunity to live a fully energized, clarified, full duration of life if we choose to care for our health, instead of depending on the health care system. Unfortunately, the health care system is set up to deal with sickness and disease after the fact, not health and wellness along the journey of life. That is up to us, and only us.

The good news here is that by taking good care of our health, we can contribute financially by minimizing the care we need from the system. Aside from heredity, accidents, and rare cases, health care costs could be substantially reduced if we simply controlled what we put into our bodies. This alone would provide ample funds for sustainable solutions, lower costs, and broader-reach benefits. It's no accident that the "Standard American Diet" spells S.A.D. With approximately one-third of our population obese and another third standing to lose a fair amount of weight, America is eating and drinking its way into mild or chronic disease and depression that costs the health care industry hundreds of billions each year. Add the financial repercussions of smoking, alcohol, and drug abuse to the mix and you could make a serious dent in world hunger. There are too many benefits of taking control of our own health to ignore it.

Consider your contribution to your life and to others by considering your health habits today.

- *Who am I counting on to take care of my health?*
- *Is how I govern my health worth ignoring until it's too late?*

It's amazing how new the same old things can become.

Isn't it time you gave your life that new-car smell?

Seventy-seven years. That's the average duration of human life according to national averages, give or take a few years. Of course, what we do with that time is our decision, and how exciting or how boring our life is comes down to choice. But life, with all of its urgencies and distractions, can and generally does sidetrack any planning to make life more fulfilling. The result is that our excitement level goes from vibrant colors to drab beige, begging the thought that comes to mind from time to time: "This is it? This is life?" Although the thought may hit us on rare occasions, we probably won't wake up one day and totally reengineer our life. It's not realistic, nor do we have to change everything. By looking at our daily routines, monthly commitments, and annual big things we do, we have amazing capacity to integrate a little innovation that can make the same-old, same-old—new, and never the same again.

It's amazing how far little adjustments can go in making life seem completely revitalized. Replace TV time with watching a learning video, dinner at the table with dinner at the park, a walk around the neighborhood with a walk on the beach, reading the paper with starting that "elusive hobby," a half-baked commitment at work with a full-court press, a day of yard work with a day of helping the neighbor with their yard, the annual timeshare in Vegas for one in the mountains . . . and so on. It's not a complete overhaul, but these small shifts in how, when, and the way we do things will take an existence that has become drab and bring a great deal more color and excitement to life.

Start a new life by doing the same old thing a little differently today.

- *Has my life become monotonous, recycled, and devoid of excitement?*
- *What activities could be adjusted to give my life more meaning and more fun?*

Leaders who don't like what they see in their team should look in the mirror.

From leaders who steer a small committee, to the upper echelon of leadership including CEOs and captains of industry, it's common knowledge that the head of the initiative or enterprise is the one responsible for the outcomes. But most leaders, including myself, will from time to time place blame on those around us for the results that are less than what we expect. Rather than accept full responsibility for the results, we disperse percentages of blame to others, and that diminishes our capacity to lead by whatever percentage we blame. Not that poor performance is to be tolerated; terminating and training are part of leadership as well. But the buck stops with leadership, and having branded hundreds of companies, I've never seen a company culture that isn't a mirror of its leader, my own included.

So where to start? Nothing in a leader or a company can be changed as fast as commitment or attitude—not technology, infrastructure, or facilities. What can change the quickest is the mind-set and behavior of the leader. When the leader commits to inspire by example and show exemplary commitment, the employees will move to mirror that behavior, and the right changes will drive a more intimate culture, greater performance, and higher stakeholder satisfaction. When the leader begins to show signs of disconnecting, blaming, and dictating rather than enrolling and inspiring, the cultural shifts (although subversive at first) will manifest in mutiny, and the end of what once was *is near.*

> ### Consider how others are following you as a direct reflection of your leadership today.

- *Do I tend to blame when results are in question, or do I look in the mirror?*
- *What ongoing tools could I implement to check my leadership results?*

Never have a phobia about phobias.

If we're afraid of losing something or getting something we don't want, then we have a phobia.

A phobia is a subtle to chronic anxiety with root causes that range from catastrophic experiences to long-term trauma to no explanation whatsoever. In most cases, they are completely unfounded. They are the parts of our DNA we wish were MIA so we could feel more A-OK. The ironic part is that everyone has phobias: death, spiders, flying, using public restrooms, computers, drinking from glass containers—there are literally thousands, and they are as bizarre as the list is long. They are rarely talked about, are concealed with great effort, and can hinder us for a lifetime without ever being brought into the light.

But there's hope. Cracking the hardened shell of phobias begins by embracing them as a provision, trusting that they will be used for some purpose in your life and the lives of others . . . and they will. Next is to get vulnerable and share your phobias with trusted friends or counsel. With every conversation, the stronghold weakens, new perspectives abound, and any shame associated can dissipate. Great work is completed in the open sharing of our issues, and you'll open others up to share about theirs as well. Studying the phobia and connecting with others who struggle with the same issue is another step to loosening its grip, as are small, incremental steps of exposure to the phobia. Together, these approaches are a deadly combination for beating phobias into submission, even killing them altogether. Although more of a journey of healing rather than an event, it can be done.

Make a little progress on your phobias today, and tomorrow and the next day.

- *Are there phobias I've been unwilling to share with others?*
- *Will I Google my particular phobia(s) today and see what comes up?*

Life gets really interesting when the acronyms are after you!

FBI, CIA, DMV, CDC, CHP, IRS, DEA, FDA, LAPD . . .
In case you haven't noticed, there's no shortage of stress in life. Life creates it, others facilitate it, the media exacerbates it, time perpetuates it, and we have a tendency to accelerate it. They have acronyms for the stress as well . . . and yet we are in the driver's seat at SCC—Stress Command Central. How much, who, and what we let in are largely our responsibility, and there are certain stresses we can avoid, some of which are the acronyms of life. They lie in wait for us to cross the line, slight the system, or break the law. And although we may see them as Big Brother, or whatever other term, phrase, or expletive we use to describe them, they are there for our own good. I can't believe I just said that, but down inside, it's true for me, and probably for us all: when in times of need, the acronyms are there to help.

But when you stray from the path of integrity with the FBI, CIA, DMV, CDC, CHP, IRS, DEA, FDA, LAPD, and other acronyms, life can take a bad turn. Remember the reference to "render to Caesar the things that are Caesar's." It means adhere to the law and pay your taxes, and it's valid for good reason. You may not like the rules from time to time, and it may be a hassle to deal with them, but there is great wisdom in following them down to the detail. A ticket unattended to goes from $250 to $1,200. An IRS meeting can either be an investment of your time or a horrific time. A drink in moderation can be a nice time or it can go too far and become jail time. It's comforting to know that other than extreme cases, the acronyms are relatively harmless if you just make the effort to do your part and deal in real time with whatever comes up. Plus it's a great way to CYB (count your blessings).

Respect the acronyms today, and they'll respect you.

- *Are my behaviors or actions going to provoke any acronyms to come after me?*
- *Are there any messes that need to be cleaned up to keep the acronyms at bay?*

Nothing in the universe can take away your power to choose. Not even you!

Two things in life never cease: change and choice.

It's amazing to think that in this vast universe, amid billions of stars and planets, some of which make the earth look like a speck of dust, and with billions of people populating the planet, we have been given an innate and undeniable power to choose. We are decision-making machines; even when we choose not to choose, we are still making a distinct decision.

Choice can be the beginning of something great or the end of great things. It has no guarantees other than you get to decide on things. And even if our choice is the wrong one or a complete blunder, we can choose to learn, choose to refocus, and choose to go again.

But the most destructive decision force of all, the one that sucks life from the marrow of our potential, is choosing not to choose, knowing there are decisions to be made but choosing to sit on the sidelines of life, undecided, lifeless, and eventually hopeless. It's the choice of not choosing that brings life to a halt, quashes our potential, and creates the downward spiral of emotions that eventually leads to resignation and despair.

Sound depressing? It is, as we become nothing more than a victim of choosing not to choose, and the price we pay for that is too high. It's vital to note that choice is the most powerful of all human forces. It's more powerful than ability, talents, and giftedness; in fact, choice is the driver of all these things.

Something in your life needs a decision; don't be a victim of choosing *not* to choose today.

- *What decisions need to be made and will I make them today?*
- *Are my choices made by wisdom and foresight, or by a Vegas-style approach?*

Negative thoughts that enter your mind don't mind entering, if you don't mind.

Life has a way of being an ongoing assault on our attitude.

You may have heard it said that thoughts are things. In truth, they are not; thoughts just influence things. The reason they are held as "things" is because they are as close to being tangible without being tangible as you can get. But we control what, when, and how things enter in. At the entry of every mind, there is a gate, and at that gate, there stands a gatekeeper who holds the key to what comes in. That gatekeeper is you and you alone. There are no allies, therapists, or friends at the gate. There's just you, and negative thoughts are showing up at an alarming rate. Not only do we invent them ourselves, but newspapers, websites, TV stations, and, of course, other people are chipping away at our attitude with less than pleasant thoughts, so the gate is always under attack. But there you are, armed with nothing but the capacity to open or close the gate, depending on the thought that's in front of you.

The key before any thoughts get in is to reframe the ones that don't serve you well, contend with them, and spend enough quality time to kill them to make sure they never return to do harm again. Even if you don't kill the thoughts completely, you'll beat them up so severely that when they show up again, you'll hold them as an unworthy opponent and discard them as inconsequential. You can also rummage around, grab thoughts that have made it through the gate, and have your way with them as well.

You are the gatekeeper. Protect the gate of your mind today and it will protect you.

- *What are the common offenders of my thought life?*
- *Will I stand at the gate as a guard or leave the gate open?*

a"CC"ountability . . .

If you want to see better, more consistent results, then cc.

Whenever you delegate something to someone, it's a gamble on how well or how poorly the other will perform in your delegation. And in today's intensely ambitious world, delegations gone bad can cost our jobs, our relationships, and precious resources. One of the bigger reasons people perform poorly or don't deliver at all is because only one person (the delegator) is aware of the delegation. So if the job ends up substandard or not done at all, there's only one set of eyeballs on the breakdown and only one repercussion to deal with. There are simply not enough people in the know to drive greater accountability and put the doer's reputation or more at stake.

To drive the point home, imagine being fifty pounds overweight, in Toastmasters, and every month you give a talk on health with the first one promising all hundred people that you will lose fifty pounds in six months. Now imagine your spouse, your children, your parents, your friends, and others you care about showing up at that first talk and every talk thereafter. Now feel the accountability and how it goes from back-of-mind to stamped-on-your-forehead for all to see. It's like wearing a sandwich board that says, "Ask me if I've lost 50 lbs"—the idea of retreating to laziness and breaking your commitment disappears, just like the weight will.

The cc function in our email box is no different and is there for many reasons, most of which are utility, some of which are strategic. I use it for accountability and a public profession of things that are going to be done. Having run a large ad agency, I remember emailing tasks to a person and cc'ing multiple parties that were stakeholders on the project. I remember what happened and had to deal with less of what didn't, all because of greater accountability.

Use the cc function so you can function better today.

- *Do I use the cc function or is it an underutilized asset?*
- *Will I be aware in each delegation of the right parties to cc? This is essential.*

No matter what level you're at in life, the next level is *waiting.*

The challenge with achieving levels of success in life is the temptation to get comfortable at any one level.

If you're alive, and I assume at this moment that's the case, then you are at a level in every area of your life. Perhaps there are levels you're content with, and perhaps there are ones you've been at too long and it's time to put forth the effort it takes to move to new heights. In either case, consider what my dad used to say: "Well, my boy, even if you just want to stand still in life, you still have to be growing." He also used to say, "Go mow the lawn," but that's another story.

Humans were not meant to stop growing, except physically, and in today's complex world it is evident that if you're not moving to the next level mentally, physically, relationally, or corporately, you'll get stuck and the steps to the next level will become that much higher. The trap of sitting on the sidelines or parking at a level too long is that with each passive day, habits of complacency harden and life becomes a spectator sport that has no real players, no cheering, and no winners. But the biggest trap of sitting at a level for too long is looking back on what you achieved, only to have the adrenaline and excitement of that success dissipate . . . and it doesn't take much time for that to happen—usually a matter of months. Before too long your future begins to look like the past that has lost almost all, if not all, of its impact.

Move to the next level today.

- *What areas of my life stopped growing, and is my current level maxed out?*
- *What would the next level look like in those areas?*

For greed, the well is never deep enough, the material things never quite enough. Greed devours itself from the inside out until there is nothing left to be satisfied.

Greed isn't good. Greed doesn't work.

We come into this world with no fancy jewelry, no nice homes, no high-performance cars, and no designer clothes. We come into existence with nothing but a bare essential . . . life, and the amazing opportunity to live it well. But somewhere along the way, greed rears its head—grabbing for a piece of candy, wanting another kid's toy, needing to have power over our parents, and by this time, we're about . . . oh, let's say, one year old. Thus the discontentment, the need to manipulate, lie, cheat, steal, distract, and steal again sets in. Innocently at first, but without good parenting to provide repercussions, it roots into a way of being that is so pervasive it grows to be an addiction, one that will never be content.

Greed not only impacts our lives, it impacts the world. If you think about it, the real problems we have in the world today are based on individual agendas and greed for money, power, prestige, and things. I agree with Gordon Gekko in the 1987 movie *Wall Street* that greed is a strong driving force. But the nature of greed is to never be satisfied; it will drive us down the road to emptiness, loneliness, and anguish, and it is a motive that is unsustainable in relationship with others. Whether at work, in your family, or in your social circles, the commitment to create mutual value in relationships and maintain an "everyone wins" posture will assault greed, thereby ensuring that happiness and success are within you and will follow you wherever you go.

BTW, if you're one to subscribe to the popular old adage "Nice people finish last," consider they will outlast, outperform, and outclass anyone stuck in the need for greed and will be successful in the true meaning of the word.

**Make the world a little less greedy;
make sure everyone wins today.**

- *How often do I consider that others' needs are as important as my own?*
- *What would relationships bring forth if I were all about win-win?*

Having a conversation is like cutting a diamond: Focus improves all facets of the outcome.

Want to ruin a good conversation? Then drift or think of what you're going to say next.

We've talked about listening before, but beyond listening is focus. In my earlier years, I was so distracted during conversations that I often got caught with no response other than a blank stare, wondering—what did this person just say, how should I respond, and how the heck do I save myself from total embarrassment? Generally, I'd be some percentage in the conversation and some percentage in thought about something that had nothing to do with the conversation. The results were always a disjointed, awkward response or clumsy redirect only to do it again after their next response. Tragic! Not only were conversations infused with stress, but they never reached even a hint of their potential, and as fate would have it, over time I became more introverted, lonely, and insecure about basic social circumstances.

Then I got married. Talk about bringing gasoline to a bonfire. It was in the process of forcing my mind to stay in the conversation that I discovered the hidden gem of creating relationships, especially with my wife. And although I still get caught in the drift from time to time, I'm now able to refocus quickly. Whereas before my conversations were 50 percent in and 50 percent distracted, today I hover around 90 percent to 100 percent in. Through a bit of work and a new habit formed, I'm keenly aware that people are well pleased when I stay within the frame of the conversation. It's a benefit that keeps me from nervously switching to the "me" show—an empty stage where I alone have a disconnected, one-way monologue, ignore the audience, and no one claps. In fact, no one's really there but me—alone, afraid, and humiliated when I get caught in the drift.

Don't miss the value of being "all in" during conversations today!

- *What percentage are you in and out of conversations?*
- *What would a day of "being all in" during conversations bring to bear?*

You don't have to walk a mile in someone's shoes to understand them; a few steps will generally do.

As we get older, life seems to get more complex. It's easier to spot how crazy life can be, not just for me but for others. But when I choose to numb out and ignore what others may be going through, my effectiveness with them becomes minimal and my indifference soars at a maximum—all because of an unwillingness to empathize for a moment.

However, the more I envision the details of someone's life, the better I am able to connect to and understand them. Just a small investment of time considering their various challenges and current realities brings greater intimacy with them, whether I am in their presence or not. It postures my heart to connect on a whole new level, and it provides the confidence I need to have more influence with them.

Although it takes a little time and focus to step into someone's shoes, the improvement in the quality of the relationship is worth the stretch. Whether it's with a stranger, friend, relative, or spouse, our commitment to empathize and gain deeper understanding will deliver constant value in both personal and business relationships.

> Place importance on what is real for others today, and they will place more importance on you.

- *Where does my empathy meter start and stop? Do I even have an empathy meter?*
- *Who would benefit from me walking a few steps in their shoes?*

Those who wait before they procrastinate are a real put-off.

Welcome to Procrastinators Anonymous! We'll get started sometime in the near future. . . .

During the course of a life, every individual has dozens of dreams, things they'd like to achieve, have, or do. For some, these dreams get accomplished, for others they lie in wait, and for others they disappear into the tomb of their complacency, *never* to see the light of day. No matter how successful or accomplished an individual has become, procrastination is like a disease—you can be healthy and free of it one moment, and in the next, it can show up and stay for a while, or a lifetime.

So why do people procrastinate? Because like everything we do, negative acts have a payoff, even negative things like procrastination. But payoffs can be deceptive and almost invisible at times, simply because we don't want to invest time to look at the payoff, let alone the impact that delaying our dreams has on our lives, or even the lives of others. The payoff of procrastination, for example, is the temporary postponement of work, pain, or stress, when in fact the effects of habitual delay of our dreams and goals can have implications that induce a number of negatives. Insecurity, pessimism, and hopelessness all grow with each postponement, all because it becomes more important to maintain our illusion of control, security, and comfort. Procrastination is not just the thief of our time; it robs our confidence, our momentum, and ultimately . . . our potential in life.

Stop procrastinating today. It's as simple as that.

- *Are the payoffs for putting things off better than actually getting things done?*
- *What are the critical events, goals, and visions I've been putting off for so long?*

Risk it, then task it.
If you don't . . . you live life in a casket.

No risk. Know failure.

I speak a lot on risk because it is foundational to everything around us. The cars, cures, machines, causes, clothes, foods, drinks, inventions, virtually everything that has impact in our life was created because someone had the courage to take a step out on a limb. In fact, if there was no risk, we would all be sitting on a big ball of dirt and water playing Tiddlywinks. Whoops, sorry—no risk, no Tiddlywinks. Actually, we'd be twiddling our thumbs, waiting around for some brave soul to make a bold move. Risk is critical, and with every risk taken, there is an opportunity to lose something or look foolish; otherwise, there'd be no risk. But risk is often misunderstood. It's not as terminal as we think in contrast to not risking. It's a simple matter of math in terms of time: The impact of failure lasts for a moment, but the ongoing fear of risking failure lasts a lifetime. It's wise to take note of the compounding danger of a play-it-safe lifestyle, as every week that goes by without risk builds the walls of limitation a little higher.

Risking is very much like exercising. The atrophy of our confidence sets in if we are not taking risks on a regular basis. If we are not consistently stretching ourselves to increase our capacity, the confidence-equity from past successes will dwindle into a lifestyle of playing not-to-lose, ensuring a life of uncertainty, apathy, and weariness. That's just too big a price to pay to avoid a little up-front fear that disappears in the early stages of the risk.

Live a little and risk today!

- *What are the areas of my life that are stuck and in need of a calculated risk?*
- *Will I think through the risk before stepping in today?*

Most divorces happen *before* marriage.

Date well or divorce soon.

Everyone has a view of dating. Some think it's fun; for others it's agony. Regardless of where you fall on the emotional date-o-meter, it remains among the most important activities of your life. Dating is a testing ground for what is to come but is often overshadowed by a "keep it on an even keel, be on my best behavior, don't be fully myself" way of being simply to make sure the other person still likes me. Add to that our avoidance of uncovering who the other person really is and you have a courtship that is built on subtle lies, withholds, and manipulation—a foundation of rubbish. It's unfortunate, but a high percentage of marriages that end are simply victims of how they began. Couples have a tendency to move too quickly, not creating the space to get to know each other's strengths and—more important—their weaknesses, pet peeves, quirks, and those proverbial skeletons. So fun becomes confused with a bond, and sex becomes confused with love, clouding whether there's true friendship or not. The comfort of just having someone to be with becomes more valuable than a journey of discovery of who the person really is and who you really are when you're with this person.

Marriage would stand more chance of survival and children wouldn't suffer as much if it were accepted that the dating relationship has a single purpose other than sex, fun, and conversation. The real purpose of dating is to qualify every aspect of the other for a lifetime, owning the truth that divorce is often a consequence of the heart saying "I think I do" just before the vocal cords say "I do."

If you're married, consider passing this on to someone who's dating today.

- *Is my dating relationship about ignoring reality or discovering what is true?*
- *What conversations, activities, and circumstances can I facilitate to get to know who it is I'm dating?*

Let's not kid ourselves:
The skeletons in our closet have a heartbeat . . .
ours!

Sharing deep truths with someone is nerve-racking in the moment. Keeping these truths inside provides a lifetime riddled with fear.

Somewhere during life we determine it's unsafe to share what really goes on inside our head, and we can be even more fearful to share what shows up in our hearts. So for many, a lifelong commitment began to share little or nothing for fear of being hurt, misunderstood, or judged. Although valid concerns, others' opinions are trivial compared to the value of letting what is bottled up on the inside reveal itself to the outside. To share or not to share—that is the quandary.

But to understand the impact of unshared baggage, take a moment to consider that every hidden feeling, judgment, and insecurity that exists in our life is slowing us down, getting us down, and keeping us down. They cast an undue burden on our mind-set and, if concealed long enough, can even have physical repercussions. Now consider that sharing realities with trusted people who can advise or simply be a listening ear in confidence may be a quantum leap in removing the weight of the baggage we carry, and a skeleton on occasion.

There are many lies about sharing our unique truths. One lie is that our issue may be bigger, scarier, and more intense than the ones that exist with those with whom we share. This is just a mental invention. Another mental invention is that others won't understand our unique brand of messed-up.

Well, no matter what the issues are, we can all relate at some level despite the different ways our issues manifest. We *all* are broken—some in different ways than others, but few really much more than others.

**Consider sharing something you think you
can't with someone you trust today.**

- *What hidden areas of my life could be shared with a trusted friend or adviser?*
- *Might being more truthful with others allow them to be more truthful with me?*

Work on your weaknesses and watch your strengths fade away. Work on your strengths and watch your weaknesses fade away.

What if working too much on weaknesses were in itself a weakness?

We all have weaknesses, and for those who think they don't, well . . . that might just be one of them. Some weaknesses we can understand, some we really can't grasp why they exist, while others will be revealed as life unfolds. Regardless, they show up at the most inconvenient times and can be a real nuisance, depending on how we contend with our weaknesses. Most of the time, we're quick to slam ourselves when weaknesses show up. We focus so intently on getting rid of the weakness that the strengths we have—those bits of brilliance that shine—sit idling while we do everything in our power to deal with idiosyncrasies that never seem to go away, all because society puts relentless pressure on us to eliminate our weaknesses. There's a billion-dollar book, CD/DVD, and training industry trying to convince us that getting rid of ineptitudes is going to improve our life. And it will, but not nearly as much as working on our strengths. When we work on our strengths, and they are functioning well and generating results, our weaknesses don't disappear; they just become irrelevant, even laughable at times. They disappear into the landscape and eventually off the canvas of our life, while the picture of our strengths becomes more focused, vivid, and complete. The real danger in life is never our weaknesses showing up here and there. The real danger is when our strengths are sidelined while we feverishly try working on the things that will have little bearing on anything substantive. It's when our strengths aren't developing that our weaknesses become so apparent.

> **Max out your strengths today
> and watch your weaknesses fade away.**

- *Do I spend more time and energy working on my weaknesses or my strengths?*
- *In what ways can I improve the impact of my strengths?*

Funerals: just one more evaluation of how we lived out our life.

Sometimes it's the RIP that reveals whether we've done A-OK. Throughout life we will experience multiple measures of how well we did—personally and professionally. Although a bit morbid, yet true, one measure of the impact we make during our lifetime will be found after life ends in how many people show up at our funeral and the way those who attend participate. To pull people away from their busy schedules to pay their respects and show support is a true indication of our "life influence and impact," even as we lay in the casket, urn, or memory. It's one of many indicators that reveal a person's reach, influence, and value during their time on earth.

But few people ever carry their thoughts out that far—to consider what exactly it is that I leave behind when I leave this place, and what memories and impact will live on in the hearts and minds of those I knew. Some people leave this planet with their financial affairs a mess, and some even leave debt behind for others to pay. Some leave a trail of broken relationships that create painful memories and a host of lifelong question marks for the survivors.

The legacy we leave at passing is one that is rarely considered, but it would benefit us and those within our care and influence to look at what it is we are leaving behind. It's not abnormal, but as we get older and attend more funerals, we'll probably get curious from time to time about how many people will come to our funeral and what the tone and manner of our funeral will be. One might even say we're dying to find out.

Take some time to think about your legacy today.

- *If I were to die today, what legacy would I leave behind?*
- *Are there financial matters, relationships, or other areas that need my attention?*

People speak the truth in percentages.

Ahhhh, little white lies. Tragically, the only thing little about those little lies is the person delivering them! But can we really be 100 percent honest? I can only imagine a world where everyone said what they thought, at full volume, in full color, regardless of who was present. Amusing to say the least; refreshing—probably so as long as there was a sensitivity to share the truth in a way that would be received by the audience. But that kind of truth is rare, because it comes at the price of someone bold enough to take the heat, deal with the repercussions, or engage in debate. And yet refined truth-telling makes truth-tellers valuable assets in society and in relationships.

But as with human nature, even truth-tellers deliver honesty in percentages and are at a level of truth during every conversation . . . from 100 percent down to 0 percent. They just happen to be comfortable at higher levels of authenticity than most. Based on our comfort level, the importance of the situation, and our own willingness to be transparent, we can become so ingrained in manipulating truth that even *we* begin to buy into our subtle deceptions. Unfortunately, our memory is rarely good enough to keep track of all those "small fabrications" of truth.

On the flip side, people of solid character are willing to consistently risk high levels of honesty to drive realization, transformation, and progress. But you can't always just vomit truth. Certain truths must be delivered with grace, compassion, and care. Truth will always bring value when one reflects deeply on when, where, and how it will best be received.

Speak the truth with care today, but speak it!

- *Do I either exaggerate or hold back my truth to others?*
- *How free would I feel if I became totally honest and graceful in my approach?*

Do you suffer from W.I.I.H.A.A.B.S.D.S?*
(Wonder If I Have An Acronym-Based Stress Disorder Syndrome)

Investigate before you medicate, or it may anesthetize what needs to be realized!

Mood-altering medications, including stimulants and antidepressants, have been around for a long time but began to be publicized a couple decades ago. In the early stages, these powerful medications were used primarily to take people with almost no functionality to a baseline of normal health so they could be in a position to receive counseling and support. Medications were used mostly in extreme cases and were dispensed with ample consideration and evaluation. Patients were kept under rigorous supervision while taking them. Today, mood-altering medications are available to almost anyone, at just about any age, with a fragment of evaluation, for just about any condition, and under anemic supervision. And these drugs, many as powerful as heroin, are often given out like aspirin with no in-depth inquiry or consideration for the actual condition being treated. In fact, many are given out with nothing more than a thirty-minute consultation, if that.

I believe that medications have a key role in helping with certain adult and child psychological cases, but in my opinion, it is dangerous to take "normal life struggles" and label them as syndromes, conditions, and disorders. I suffer from W.I.L.D., Waiting In Line Disorder. Perhaps someday they'll invent Slozac—the cure for those experiencing tension in slow-moving lines. I know this may offend some, but please read it with the heart I intend and that is this: It would be wise to consider every conceivable option, including diet, exercise, education, and counseling, before taking medication today . . . any medication.

Consider all the options before taking medications today.

- *Would I consider diet, exercise, education, and counseling before medications?*
- *Am I clear about the repercussions of taking medications long-term?*

*NOTE: I am not a doctor and I do see the value in the use of mood-altering medications in a closely supervised environment and/or counseling. However, the "dispense it like aspirin" practices coming from some of the medical profession should be under greater scrutiny.

It's hard to set the world on fire when the world is wet.

Not too long ago, the technical revolution created a wave of economic growth that was equivalent to, if not greater than, that of any other revolution. The growth had nothing to do with who was in government at the time but was the result of people embracing a new direction and contributing their innovation. The economy was white-hot, with money flowing like a river.

Well, the wave of that revolution has subsided, and the government has amassed a debt load that the mind can barely comprehend. Money is now flowing like sludge.

Regardless of who is to blame, the true consequences of our debt have yet to be seen. I don't have an economics degree or a political background, but I suspect we are not coming out of difficult times but going deeper in. This is not a doomsday mentality but instead the result of a combination of statistics, facts, figures, global realities, and of course my instinct. Whether or not I'm right, it would serve us well to be good stewards of our finances and resources. Controlling costs and setting budgets is hard on our lifestyles, and our pride. But so is restoring bad credit, getting out of debt, and not having the funds available when great opportunities come along . . . and trust me, they will. We can't predict what the future holds, but we can sharpen our skills, thinking, and disciplines to do life more creatively and strategically so we can remain solvent financially—you know, the way we'll need to be to set the world on fire when it dries off.

Consider the long-term realities as you handle your resources today.

- *Am I in touch with the realities of our global economic system?*
- *Is there room to be more strategic regarding when, where, and how I use resources?*

If you want people to value what you say, capture *not* their ears but their imagination.

Words. It seems the older we get, the more powerful they must be to grab our attention.

With so many avenues of communication today, the competition to be heard is fierce, and merely opening our mouths and speaking is no longer a viable option to ensure others will listen. It's flattering to think people are glued to every word we say, but it's also self-deception if we don't pay close attention to the impact of our communication and whether it creates the intended results. Often we are so casual about our communications that our low level of intentionality makes others want to end the conversation rather than engage further. Another "go nowhere" conversation strikes again.

I have to imagine that if I'm getting tired of hearing myself talk, others may be too. Instead of speaking to people in our canned vernacular or within our comfort zone, we can integrate foresight and innovation so they don't just hear our words but are *moved* by them. We have opportunities in conversation to play a little and to break the patterns of recycled verbiage, to tune in to others so we don't just talk to them but *captivate* them.

Put some imagination in your verbalization today.

- *Are my conversations becoming too repetitive to be heard?*
- *Will I consider that capturing others' imagination is a key to progress?*

When someone breaks their commitment to you and doesn't authentically show remorse, it's not personal, it's a cry for help!

If you look deep enough, underneath a broken promise you'll find a broken heart.

All of us have experienced broken commitments from those around us, thousands of them over a lifetime. As a result, today's value on keeping promises and our faith in humankind to deliver on what they say is at an all-time low, and flakiness is more common today than in any other time in history. But how we process broken commitments is a real issue, as we usually default to a couple of options: Get mad, which eats us up inside, or get even, which starts a war. If we took a moment to uncover what was behind someone's broken promise, we might move to compassion rather than judgment and move in to help rather than move on. Fact: People who don't keep their word with others are in serious trouble, as breaking commitments is not a compartmentalized practice. It's a character flaw that generally shows up everywhere in a person's life and is a condition of the heart where commitments are governed by feelings, not by character.

The question becomes: Who will step in to confront the breakdown? Who will dare to make a difference? In today's tiptoe-around-the-issues, don't-ruffle-any-feathers world, it is rare and refreshing when someone steps in when we flake and addresses it with grace and a forthright heart. These are true friends, bold and caring enough to lovingly interrupt the things that don't work in our lives. Some people never discover the repercussions of their broken commitments, because so few have the courage to confront them. Perhaps this is why breaking commitments is at a pandemic state in this world.

Address broken commitments head-on, but make sure your heart is on as well.

- *Who do I know who consistently breaks commitments? Will I step in to help?*
- *What percentage of both small and large commitments do I keep?*

Resig "Nation"

A re you aligned to a worthy cause, or resigned to just point out flaws? Our country is quickly becoming a nation resigned to the idea that we are a victim of our government. Conversations ensue and complaints abound that we are powerless to influence changing the things we see. But if we took inventory of our own lives, we'd find some of the grievances we have with government are alive and well in our own actions: personal agendas, evading truth, being greedy for power and possessions, overspending, bending the rules, slighting taxes, manipulating the system, capitalizing on the system, etc. This is where the hypocrisy begins. Rather than look in the mirror at our own behavior and how it is affecting "our world" and "the world," we conveniently keep our own contribution, or lack thereof in most cases, out of our political conversations to save face. So for sport and to vent our own frustrations, we throw conversational darts at the government, trying to give our perspectives to solve the world issues when we should be focusing on our own issues. Those who realize "We are a government of the people" understand that governing themselves and their relationships into "collective good" doesn't leave time or energy to gripe about how bad things are. It's a lifetime work where governing our own behavior determines whether or not we wake up every morning and contribute life into the world or suck life out of it. The country could change in a second if everyone got off their political high horses and began governing their own lives according to the principles this country was founded upon, including hard work and self-sacrifice. It's personal responsibility that makes up the collective whole . . . without it we wind up in the collective hole.

**Focus on self-government
as the nation's biggest possibility today.**

- *Am I more into degrading the government or into exercising self-government?*
- *What will I bring that is different to my next political conversation?*

Are you in the habit
of habitually ignoring the value of habits?

Fortunately and unfortunately, you cannot *not* have habits. Habits are open for business 24/7. The question becomes: "Are my habits serving the goals I have or stopping them? Are they contributing positively to the relationships in my life or causing stress and relational turmoil? Are they building my confidence or tearing me down?"

Conducting a simple habit inventory could give you an answer pretty quickly. Take out some paper and draw a line down the middle. On one side write down your good habits; on the other side write the bad ones. Make sure you cover all areas of your life. Once you identify the good ones, you'll be able to see clearly how they benefit your life and how doing more of them will yield even better life results. Once you identify the bad ones, you'll understand how eliminating those bad habits would create the opportunity to put more time and effort into the good habits. Consider that today you have habits you need to break and ones you need to create. Also consider that your life will be the same or radically different three, six, nine, twelve months from now, depending on the habits removed and the ones integrated.

Habits are the life-force of progress, and they make and break just about everything. Yet we rarely take inventory of our habits or the effects they are having on our relationships, career . . . even our mental health. Experts say it takes between twenty-one and thirty-one days to form or break a habit. They also say the growth you'll experience this year will depend on the people you meet, the books you read, and the habits you form. I believe that habits are the strongest of the three; they are foundational to everything, *even meeting people and reading books. . . .*

Consider the habit of how you relate to habits today.

- *Am I in the habit of checking on my habits or aloof to what they are?*
- *Which of my bad habits is causing the most grief in my life?*

The thirst for knowledge is a good thing until it starves life.

I s it that you need to learn more or just apply what you already know? In today's information age there is no shortage of knowledge. As I shared earlier, the same amount of information that had been delivered into society since the beginning of time until about the year 2005 is now delivered into the world every forty-eight hours. Add to that what we learned in school, from our parents, books we've read, and people we've learned from, and it's safe to say that we know the essentials. If by the time a child is about four years old their view of life is formed, then by twenty-one we must know a thing or fifty about life. But knowledge not applied is knowledge that died. Hence, adding knowledge on top of knowledge for knowledge's sake can be overrated and unproductive. What is constant, though, is the clear need for us to diligently apply the things we do know: the basics, like treating others the way we want to be treated, keeping every commitment we make, creating value for others, and things that have nothing to do with information but make us great human beings and the most sought-after people on the planet. The trap of the "knowledge quest" reveals that by the time we remember to put into action that which we recently learned, we will be barraged and distracted with another life-changing trend that may seem more attractive. That trend will soon be replaced with the latest and greatest life-changing paradigm that we will start to apply, only to be sidetracked again with the latest fad of personal development . . . and another life-changing principle is on its way. It's not that we need to know more to grow more, it's that we should focus on what we already know, apply it to its fullest, and reap the rewards of application.

Apply what you know to the fullest today!

- *What one thing do I already know that needs to be put into action?*
- *How do I use the quest for knowledge to escape what I know needs to be done?*

Use your head and don't let your mouth get ahead of your head.

Our words will have more power when we exercise power over our words.

You won't find many books, TV shows, or seminars dedicated to the topic of verbal self-control. Maybe that's because as humans, we feel a sense of entitlement to say whatever it is we want to say, regretfully at times. Verbal restraint is one of those character traits we wish we'd exercised, oh, about a million times by the time we hit eighteen, but for some, it continues over a strifetime—I mean lifetime. Our mouths have this innate capacity to get us into trouble quicker than an exhale, and yet the topic doesn't get much attention. They don't teach it in school, where self-control gone bad is often dealt with in the form of reprimand or punishment, with little time explaining the value of this elusive and uncommon trait.

With rare exception, everyone I've met in my life would like to be wiser, smarter, more attuned, and more effective in relationships—personal or business. Restraint in communication through more listening and watchfulness has the ability to improve these areas faster than an inhale. The insights, intelligence, and value we attain from a bit of caution pay big in a world of verbosity and frivolous words. And let's face it, nobody has the patent on self-control. Except perhaps for the rare one-in-a-billion monk sitting on a rug in the mountains, it's not a trait we typically master. But as we work on self-control, which often shows up in the things we don't say, we will begin to see that the long-term value far outweighs the desire to shoot off our mouths for a brief moment in any given situation.

Practice self-control and see what *doesn't* happen today.

- *When does my lack of self-control show up, and what problems does it cause?*
- *What could life be like with more well-thought-out conversations?*

Belief: that little thing that makes big things possible.

It's nice to know we can go from no faith, to low faith, to total faith in a matter of seconds.

Have you ever considered what makes an athlete a superstar? Most athletes will tell you that at some point in their career, they had a shift in their mind-set that changed everything—a truly transformational moment. Nothing *physical* changed, because for most athletes, their actual ability is something that improves in fractional percentages over time. But giant leaps in ability happened when their *belief* system shifted and their current physical ability became supercharged. Contracts got signed, salaries got tripled, records were set, and Hall of Fame status was just around the corner.

Although we're not all professional athletes, the same holds true for mere mortals—moms, dads, workers, business professionals, pastors, teachers, volunteers, and the like. Regardless of vocation or location, strengthening our belief system is life's biggest opportunity, and learning to tune our "belief engine" can be the difference between a life filled with starts and stops or one filled with progress, momentum, and true greatness. It can take the ordinary to the extraordinary and bring about a confidence that will impact every area of life. Belief is among the few things you have the power to change, and the intensity of your beliefs will drive ideas to become a reality. Belief doesn't always determine the actual outcome, but ask anyone who ever achieved anything great, and at the core of their story you'll find *belief* was the impetus to initiate action, knock down walls, silence naysayers, and keep momentum.

Spend some time talking yourself into greatness today instead of out of it.

- *Where do my beliefs stop or slow me from achieving great results?*
- *Who or what can I depend on to help strengthen my belief system?*

Shining light upon ourselves only puts others further in the dark.

During our interaction with others, the temptation to shed light on who we are, the value we bring, what we are selling, and what we've accomplished seems to weasel its way into many a conversation . . . sometimes a bit too soon, and a bit too much. Truth is, those are not conversations, they're often just a personal brand pitch, bringing an overabundance of light on ourselves, while the other contemplates a way out of the darkness. If we are in the habit of these "me-focused" conversations, the idea of putting the spotlight on the other, showing genuine interest and bringing light to their life plays second fiddle to our insecure need to broadcast the plus side of our human balance sheet. The problem with one-way conversations like these is when they end, it leaves the other empty, tired, and realizing anything they say will pale in comparison to the big pile of conversational dung, just thrown in their face. There is nothing impressive about that, and there never will be. But to be fascinated with others by drawing out who they are, and discovering *their* value, brings light and a lightness to the conversation that is nothing short of beautiful. Not to mention, at the end of discovering others and putting the spotlight on them, we get discovered for who we are in the process; giving, listening, caring, unconventional, and rare.

**Put the light on others today,
you'll be brighter because of it.**

- *Would the stress of conversations be minimized if I got out of performance mode?*
- *How much more would I learn about others if I were to inquire more and talk less?*

Don't let your anticipation of the future rob the value that exists in the present.

Ironically, having a vision can actually be a poison to the present. As I alluded to earlier, every powerful thing has two sides. One is the value it provides; the other is when it goes too far and becomes a weakness or an obstacle. For example, a vision for the future is a great thing until it blurs the value and possibility of what's in the present. It can make all things in real time seem meaningless or irrelevant. The result is people and things become nothing more than a way to get what you want, and you begin the process of using people rather than loving and caring for them in ways that matter.

In almost every successful visionary's life, you'll find a common theme: "I was so wrapped up in my future, I missed the relationships that mattered most. That was my life's biggest failure, and all the money in the world can't buy back what was lost." Seems like quotes like this are infused in just about every successful person's biography ever written. Unfortunately, it's usually the family that pays the price. Somehow in the trance and execution of the vision, life balance gets shelved, and having a life where all things are maturing and in good health seems impossible. The result is usually that one area grows full-steam ahead, while the others become collateral damage.

The idea that *all* things in your life can grow at the same time with no one thing spiking at the expense of the others is possible if you're willing to view balanced growth as life's biggest success, even more specifically, if you view it as your vision.

Consider the concept of "all things growing" in your life today.

- *What one area of my life is dominating while the others may be suffering?*
- *Do I tend to drift out of the present and miss the beauty of what is in front of me?*

From the moment a couple says "I do," the relationship begins to die.

Sometimes it doesn't take long for "I do" to become "I might" or "I won't."

I've been challenged on the concept of the "instantly withering marriage," but once I convince the debater that human nature will always bend to itself no matter which way it bends, parties concur that time is an enemy of keeping couples together, and that marriages decline from the words "I do." Couples soon find out that the walk down the aisle is not a walk in the park, which makes marriage prey for human nature to do its thing. When married couples start out, each spouse has a marriage bank account of love, trust, and commitment. And at the time of marriage, the account balance is usually at its peak. But with every snide comment, mess left on the table, lie, betrayal, concealment, hurtful statement, argument, etc., the account loses a little relational equity and the balance goes down. Depending on how full the account was at the beginning of marriage, it may not be able to handle many withdrawals before it becomes anemic, overdrawn, or bankrupt. The key is not only to reduce the relational withdrawals, as that alone will not sustain a marriage, but also to bring relational deposits of love, trust, care, and valuing the other to the marriage, preferably through many small deposits throughout the day, rather than letting the account dwindle down to nothing and thinking a single large deposit will fill up the account. It doesn't work that way. There will be ups and downs, no doubt, but the goal is to have the account balance bounce up and down between amazing and healthy. Couples can bounce all life long with that balance. The marriage gets into trouble when it bounces between status quo and near empty. In that zone, it only takes one bounce to close out the account.

Keep the marriage account healthy.
Make some relational deposits every day.

- *What is the account balance in your marriage, engagement, or dating relationship?*
- *What things can I do to bring the account to a healthier level?*

Your talent will endure hardship where there is lack of relationship.

People won't listen to you because of your ability but because of your relatability. I've known many highly intelligent, incredibly gifted people who seem to have a tough go at making progress. You probably know some too. The talents are there in abundance, but the relational skills and the limited ability to communicate in a way that works makes for many casualties.

So if progress really exists in power of relationships as much as in talents, why is there so little emphasis today on how to effectively resonate with others? The real reason is that if we have abilities of any substance, we tend to lean toward a prideful posture of "If I speak, others should listen," regardless of manner, tone, or content. As an example, the apostle Paul in the Bible was among the most gifted men of his time. You'd think if he showed up to a meeting, people would listen. And they did. Not because he was brilliant, though, but because he was relevant. Paul invested forethought prior to conversations, meetings, and gatherings. He became clear about *whom* he was going to be speaking with and adjusted his communication style, his dress, and his content to ensure that those he was with would be approached in a way that worked for *them* and *their* specific life circumstances. He went to great lengths to consider what a relatable style would be and grounded himself before entering in. He was about making an intimate connection, creating trust, and valuing others as the precedent for every encounter. In turn, people felt valued and respected, and they opened their minds and hearts to listen to his brilliance.

Focus on your relatability more than your actual ability today.

- *How much forethought goes into the conversations and meetings I have?*
- *Are my talents and abilities being hindered because of my relatability?*

During tough times in life, it's easy to medicate ourselves with distraction.

The worst state to live in is the state of distraction.

If you look at the state of world affairs, you will be certain of one thing—*nothing is certain.* The changes in the way we do business and our global capacity to cross continents through technology mean things will be forever changed, and to a large degree questionable, because so much is moving beyond our control. These shifts demand that we bring a new level to our focus and bring new disciplines into practice to minimize distractions. Due to heightened stress levels that come with economic downturns and changes in world affairs, we sometimes choose to work on what we'd *like* to do, or what is *easy* to do, rather than on the work we *should be doing.* It's the deception that "busyness equals productivity," and as long as I keep going, working on the distraction, it will change the state of current realities. Trust me, it won't. Things will get worse! The truth is, there are dozens of distractions that we can medicate ourselves with, but usually just a few things that will get us where we need to be. Distraction becomes a drug of choice, an addiction that keeps us avoiding the discomfort of working on what we need to work on to get past the "stuck point." Times like these demand focus on the critical work despite inconvenience or difficulty; they also demand that we count the price we will pay if we don't work on what's important instead of what's comfortable.

Identify what's critical today, get busy, stay focused, and reap the reward.

- *What core activities will have immediate impact on my circumstances?*
- *What "medicating" things do I distract myself with daily, and why?*

Forced creativity is like speed surgery.
It gives "cutting edge" a whole new meaning.

Ever try to force innovation and strain through the creative process only to find yourself frustrated, unfulfilled, and left with nothing but mediocre ideas and a tired brain? Aside from the rare times when pressure and need birth great ideas, most innovation comes from a place of rest—not *physical* rest, but *mental* rest, where the mind is relaxed, uncluttered from the urgencies of life, left with nothing but the full capacity to think freely about what is possible. It's like freeing up memory space on your computer. For the moment, it creates opportunity for more data, it works at a faster speed, and it reduces the dreaded crash, which in the ideation world is mental overload, ideation fatigue, and quitting.

But everyone rests differently. We all have a place where our innovation soars and the anxieties of life disappear, leaving only a creative platform from which to think. For some, it's in an easy chair; others think freely at the beach; for some, a walk does the trick; for others, it's being locked in a cabin for a few days. Regardless of geography, the process of rest eliminates the rust and is effective combat against stagnancy.

As for the rewards for engaging in this space—they are nothing short of miraculous, if you take the time. But innovation time is different for everyone. Some people need a few quiet minutes; others require a half hour to wind down; others need a planning day; others need several days to find that zone. The problem is always carving out the time to get there and planning the ideation path once you arrive. Most of us have computers, others use a hard copy calendar, but the key here is to schedule "innovation time" and be blessed by what occurs there.

- *Is my innovation held hostage to a busy schedule and a cluttered mind?*
- *When and where is my unique space to think freely without stress or pressure?*

Making someone look bad in public works . . . *you* look bad!

We all do stupid things from time to time. Some we know about, some become the topic of conversation at a later date, and some we get by without anyone noticing (and are quite relieved when we do). Of course, it's one thing to do dumb things in private but altogether different when they happen in public. The embarrassment gets magnified in direct proportion to the number of eyeballs focused on the blunder.

But whenever someone falls short of what we think is appropriate in public, or they just plain screw up, we have a few different options. First, we can pretend we didn't see, which doesn't work very well, because no matter how deft we are at masking, it's still written all over our face, and with one lock of the eyeballs, it's over. Next, we can engage eye contact, give a smile and a nod of empathy (or at least sympathy), and move on as if nothing happened, as in the grand scheme of things, nothing really did happen. The third option is we can bring attention to the screwup, whatever kind of breakdown it might be. We can make fun of it, confront it, and bring unnecessary attention to it with a goal of making the other look foolish or inadequate.

FYI: Making someone look foolish in public is a strategy to make ourselves look good, either through the creative way in which we do it or by an implied comparison that we would never be so stupid to do such a thing (too late). Either way, *we* are the ones who look like the fool in those circumstances. It's in those moments where we can be either an idiot of arrogance or a hero of levity. The former causes division and resentment, the latter has the ability to create rapport and trust with others in about fifteen seconds.

Practice a little empathy to make a big difference today.

- *When I screw up, and I will, how would I like others to respond?*
- *When others make a mistake, will I be a momentary hero or zero?*

Work is only work when you're not in the rhythm of doing it.

To make progress requires hard work, but hard work requires you! More and more people are depending on sources outside themselves to sustain their lifestyles, even their existence, than in times past. The reality that we are responsible for our sustenance in life is taking a backseat to programs and assistance that are enabling perfectly healthy, capable individuals to put their life and all the value that hard work brings on hold, because for the moment it's easier than pushing past the perceived adversity. Keep in mind, I'm as cognizant and supportive of the need to help those who are incapable of helping themselves as the next human. And when I pay my taxes, I'm happy to fund programs that help those in true need. But today what we coin as "incapable, troubled, or in need" is getting looser and more pathetic by the day. Healthy, capable people who have the capacity to control their own circumstances are draining the health of the system designed to help those who truly can't. That's the tragic part. After a bit of time on earth, I'm sure you've discovered, like me, that life is hard, and whether you were raised in Harlem or in the Hamptons, each has its own level and style of difficulty and neither offers much when a life of resignation reveals itself. In the entitlement age, many have lost touch with the value of hard work. It's as though with all the technology to make things easier, life should be easier as well. But it's not. We would be wise to own the reality that as things become more difficult, we will best be prepared if we are in the rhythm of working and giving into society rather than taking resources from it. Tough words, yes! But not nearly as tough as depending on a system outside yourself that is becoming more and more anemic and eventually may be gone.

**You know what you need to do today.
Work it in. Work it out.**

• *Am I working to my full potential in life or letting my potential wither?*
• *Am I contributing more into the world than I am taking out?*

Deciding in advance of a thing will always advance that thing.

Life is composed of decisions. Good decisions = good life. Bad decisions . . . do the math!

Whenever we go into conversations where decisions will have to be made, the norm is to use the conversation as a tool to gain all the facts needed for the decision. Not a bad approach, but the tendency to engage without thinking through all the potential realities in advance is really a novice way to go. So rather than entering into the conversation where we've thought about all the potential directions and defined our decisions and responses in advance, we step in unprepared, undecided, unresolved, and uncertain about the outcomes and potential surprises. We wait for the conversation to fill in the blanks that could have been filled in before entering in.

Generally, a brief bit of time thinking on what options you'll consider and how the decision will affect you and others will drive a more specific and relevant conversation. For example, if you go in to ask for a raise, it would be wise to have the following in your quiver to pull out if and when needed: things like the value of your job position, how you've impacted the company, the ways you've gone above and beyond, the dollar value (ROI) of your contributions, what things would be like without you, the cost to the company if you were gone, etc. Now for the decision points: the exact range you'll be willing to accept (looking for $X but willing to accept $Y), the terms and timeline of the promotion, what you'll do if the range, terms, and timeline are not met. The more specific you are in advance, the better. Thinking through things in advance takes away the surprises, keeps the conversation from veering off track, and makes whoever you are conversing with take you much more seriously because you're resolved, clear, and very prepared.

**Think things through in advance today, and
you'll advance whatever the thing is!**

- *Do I wing it or go into situations with predetermined outcomes in mind?*
- *What would meetings look like if I were the most prepared one in the room?*

A shortcut rarely is. . . .

If at the end of your life you totaled up all the time you thought you saved by taking shortcuts, you'd probably be in the negative . . . in more ways than just time.

As an impatient person, my first instinct when put to task is to think about how *fast* I can get things done, not always how *right* I can get things done. That usually comes second. Not that my thinking is flawed, but more often than not, I spend more time doing it the short way, and others are impacted by my secondhand quality. I also feel that I'm gambling with my integrity. Depending on the task or initiative, risking a shortcut can mean risking safety, your job, your health, your reputation, and perhaps your life.

So meditate for a moment on the risk of shortcuts in contrast to doing it right, and consider the value of consistency in solid results and character vs. hits and misses. Idiot vs. genius is as simple as I can put it. I must admit, however, that there is an adrenaline rush that comes with crazy shortcut ideas like tying the lawn mower to a tree trunk, taping the throttle on full, and letting the mower wrap around the tree until the lawn is done. But more than likely the neighbor's flower bed winds up trashed, a car gets dented, and the lawn looks like a bad haircut. Don't get me wrong, I'm all for efficiency, but these days I'm more about effectiveness, as society's intolerance for mediocrity is growing by the day, and its demand for things to be done right is more expected than appreciated. Odds are that doing it right will always be more effective, more profitable, and more fulfilling than taking shortcuts and strengthening the bondage of impatience.

Don't let shortcuts cut short what is possible by a job well done today!

- *What shortcuts have me doing more work or negatively affect my reputation?*

- *How do my shortcuts impact other people's productivity and reputation?*

The question "What am I going to do?" will be answered when you decide "Who am I going to be?"

You've heard the old phrase "Agonize over decisions." Well, every day brings a series of "What do I do's?" to life. Some days it's small decisions, other days big issues arise that demand more attention, and sometimes either the quantity or intensity of decisions can bring a bit of agony. Any way you look at it, the number of circumstances we are faced with day-to-day make it advisable to have a consistent strategy for making great decisions.

But unless we are clear on our stand in life and in our character, making choices that align with our true self will be elusive at best. Not being sure about "what to do" over and over again is nothing more than a symptom of being uncertain about "who we are going to be" in circumstances. And because we're unsure of the "being" traits—such as being kind, gentle, committed, giving, considerate, transparent, straightforward, rational, and so on—the "what to do" options are not only vast but confusing and filled with wavering. When our character is unstable, every decision made will be based on how we *feel* in that moment rather than on our predetermined character.

Deciding on your way of being in life is foundational to all actions, and it clarifies what you will do and how you will go about life with great predictability and confidence. For example, when I am counseling and the person asks, "What should I do?" I respond with, "Well, let's start with who are you going to be in the circumstance you are in." Then I just listen to them outline their character, heart, and way of being. For example, "I will be caring, giving, humble, and coachable." When they're done identifying who they will be, I calmly ask, "So what would a person like that do?" Nearly every time, they know exactly what they'd do. Their choice is surprisingly lucid, birthed in conviction, and almost always an action that will generate the best results.

**Get clear on who you will be today
for a better today and tomorrow.**

- *Is what I do based on my feelings or on my predetermined character?*
- *Am I even clear about my own core values such that my decisions are clear?*

Arguments are not birthed from the outside in, but from the inside out.

Conflicts are internal. They reside in what already is, not in what just happened.

I would say nobody likes arguments, but there are some who *do* find them entertaining, and others who view them as sport and play to win regardless of who gets hurt. Let's just call them the rare few whom we rarely invite to dinner. This ShiftPoint is for the rest of us common folk who view an argument like getting a traffic ticket . . . better to talk our way out of it—the faster, the better. The truth is, arguments don't exist outside of ourselves, meaning you could search the entire planet with a microscope and never find an argument. One could argue that, but I'd still be right, as arguments don't exist on the earth . . . anywhere. They are, however, alive and well in our hearts and minds, and are a great eye-opener of our insecurity, selfishness, unresolved anger, lingering bitterness, or judgments. In short, most arguments are a symptom of our emotional dysfunctions, where rather than choosing to be rational and peaceful, we choose to be assaultive and destructive.

But it should also be noted that arguments themselves aren't bad, and we should be grateful when they start, as they draw out hidden bitterness, resentments, and other deficiencies we need to work on. Arguments are a clear revelation of what is really going on with us emotionally, and they draw out what is already there. The problem is that we don't want to be wrong or wronged, so we go into defense mode and the argument begins, only to end when things change on the inside. A good goal for any person is to be free from an "internal argumentative spirit." By staying in the mode of being a peacemaker instead of a peacebreaker, we push out harmful immaturities and usher in a calming presence and a caring heart; we become an instrument of healing in disagreement, not an instrument of destruction.

Get over winning arguments and you'll win people over today.

- *Do I have a predisposition to be offended?*
- *Am I more about winning arguments than winning in relationships?*

As a person thinketh, they thinketh. As a person doeth, it gets done!

Well, I know it's been on the back burner for forty years, but I'm still thinking about it.

Thinking is a great strength, but like every strength, it can become a weakness if it goes too far. Often the thinking that comes in advance of doing something is too impotent to be effective, as it is birthed in speculation, not experience, and done in distracted spurts rather than disciplined meditative thought. In this way, thinking actually becomes a liability to progress rather than an asset. Although an esoteric example, if Nike's slogan was "Just think about it" instead of "Just do it," I'd be confident in saying that fewer people would be sporting Nike's logo. Regardless, the whole success of Nike's campaign was and still is based on the premise that the value in the doing will surpass the value of sitting on the sidelines, thinking, dreaming, or even planning. Nike was wise enough to know that people need to be pushed into action, and so the tagline creates the drive and accountability to make something tangible happen. In life, there is a healthy think-do ratio wherein the moment we start to under-think or over-think a goal is about the moment we should get busy on it. For many, life is one big contemplation in which "Someday I'll do . . ." starts off as an innocent plight, only to end up as the opportunity that once was. Not to mention—the thinking that takes place while doing has ten times the power of thinking while daydreaming. Think about it . . . no, *don't*!

In the words of the #1 sports brand, "Just do it" today.

- *What do I keep thinking about over and over again that just needs to get done?*
- *What would life be like if I moved from just thinking about it to just doing it?*

Trying to quit something before you have something to replace it with is futile.

Quitting something can be easier if you have a genuine replacement part.

We all have things we'd like to quit: jobs, addictions, relationships, bad habits, quirks, fears, and more, much more. But quitting isn't easy, and quitting on quitting something is more the norm than persisting through the pain of transformation. Personally, and I speak from experience, I've always felt it nearly impossible to break any addiction, stronghold, or habit unless I replace it with something that's of equal or greater value to me. The idea of stopping any behavior without a new vision to focus on will drive the never-ending mental conversation of, "I need to quit this." *What?* "This!" *Quit what?* "This, you know—THIS!" Unfortunately, the quit-this-without-another-option strategy acts as a perpetual reminder to focus on the breakdown, not on a replacement. In order to proactively remove whatever "this" is, we need to move from *this* to *that*.

Like an engine, whatever part breaks down needs to be replaced with a part that is equal or greater in performance to keep the engine running. And like baseball, if your second baseman isn't cutting it, you can't nix the position; you have to find a better option. For example, the commitment to move away from pornography to have a great sex life with your spouse, or to move away from gluttony to get in the best shape of your life, or to quit drugs to have a clear mind for future vision. Having a vision (replacement part) that is greater than any breakdown in our life is a tool to pull us away from the breakdown we're in and draw us into new perspectives, new value, and new relationship. In other words, the more effort you put forth with the new thing, the more you'll detach from the old. It's not a guarantee, but consider the upside: even if you hold on to the old thing (which will eventually get dealt with sometime), you still get the value of investing in the new thing.

Everyone has a quit list. Quit intelligently today.

- *What would the replacement parts for my quit list look like?*
- *What one thing could I focus on quitting, and what would replace it?*

It's not the goal but working on the goal that creates the value.

Working on goals may not be everyone's flavor; it was never mine, to be honest. I always migrated toward an organic approach to accomplishing things, but now that I've set a few goals—a few turned out and others didn't—I see goals in a whole new light.

What I discovered is that there are personal and character growth qualities that exist in working on goals that are more powerful and rewarding in the long run than just about any other effort. The inherent qualities that are derived from the goal process even surpass the joy and reward of achieving the goal in the long run . . . and by a long shot. Those who've accomplished goals know that the rush, the juice, and the adrenaline of completing them end quickly.

What remains after the process of working on the goal is the real value. I now know that the process of working on any goal is the "gold" of the goal itself. Starting the goal is your excitement and passion, executing the goal becomes your teacher and wisdom, completing the goal becomes your confidence and character. The goal itself is perishable—it's tentative at best. Millions of goals that were accomplished no longer exist. The traits that come from working on a goal last a lifetime, and the qualities that we acquire through them make the next goal more predictable, attainable, and fulfilling. I call it goal momentum, and once in the flow, it's hard to stop. Start working on your goals so your goals can start working on *you.*

Start the process of building a better you by starting on a goal today.

- *How have the goals that I've achieved in the past impacted who I am today?*
- *What would be a realistic goal I could work toward in the next thirty days?*

Building relationships with others is not about doing a few big things throughout the year but a few small things every day.

The more frequently you impact others, the more they know you care.

Big problems manifest in our lives when we don't pay attention to the small things we should be doing, and the small things are bigger than we think. They bring a level of consistency in our impact with others, and they let them know that they are important and on our hearts more frequently than a couple times a year. They outweigh the big things many to one, and the big things we are often forced to do are a cover-up for the small things we're not doing.

For example, it's easy to go into lazy mode after you do something big for someone. In some way, we think doing "a big thing" for someone every now and then buys us time to go back into a relationally comatose state for a while. And when the impact of the big thing wears off a few days later, we wonder why that big thing we did isn't sustaining the relationship and the other person is feeling a lack. And then when they express the lack, we defend it by saying, "Well, what about that big thing I did?" Big things never will be catalysts for great relationships unless you're doing big things every day. The truth is, that's a bit of overkill, because it's not necessary, nor is it realistic, which leaves the small things. When it comes to keeping relationships *growing*, let alone *going*, the details are what matter; the little things that let others know we legitimately care about them and that they are front-of-mind with us. It's these little touch-points that make others—and you—feel honored, loved, and appreciated.

Do a few little things for someone today.

- *Do I ignore little things and try to buy my way out with occasional big things?*
- *Do I even know what the little things are, and might I have the courage to ask?*

The smartest people in the world are those who find smart people to ask what they don't know!

Life and its complexity are supposed to get easier as I get older. What's the deal?

As I get older, there seems to be a rapidly growing list of things that are beyond my knowledge base. Life is throwing a new smattering of age-centric circumstances, technology is changing so fast I need intravenous tech support, and business is moving from local to global every day. And yet with all the changes, the answers exist for all we need to know. They're out there. In fact, there are experts who would be willing to help in a moment's notice, as whoever is smart at something is efficient at learning, and those who learn typically love to teach.

The misconception is that people who are qualified to help and have reached a level of success in life won't have time for you. The truth is, busy people have great capacity, and mentoring someone through an issue is something those who love to teach will make time for—if you humble yourself and ask kindly. As astonishing as this is to me, I've never been turned down when asking someone for help, and I've asked a lot.

Today in your life, you need answers. We all do. Could be something simple to something that will impact the rest of your life, but there are problems, objectives, and goals where you need perspectives beyond your own. A brief time of thought will reveal a potential counselor or two, and the good news is, if there are no immediate experts in the area you need, someone you know knows someone, and so on. The bad news is that our pride or complacency can keep us from getting the help we need.

Get some feedback on something you need to know about today.

- *Who is on my A-list of trusted advisers in the areas of family, career, spirituality, etc.?*
- *What learning sites and blogs are dedicated to information I need to know?*

Whenever someone is offending you, look past their offense into their fear.

I once told someone that to be offended was a choice. They chose to be offended!

Typically, when someone betrays, offends, or interrupts our space, agenda, or life in some way, our first instinct is to judge them using our own unique brand of judgment or whatever style suits us in the moment. We conjure up all sorts of mental inventions, from the unoriginal, like ("They're an [expletive]") to some other more elaborate psychological evaluations and labels that usually have no context, proof, or sensibility—you know, the emotionally driven reactionary stuff that constantly gets us into trouble.

But what if you had the self-control to refrain from instinctive thoughts of indifference and could connect to the idea that the root of someone's offense is *never* anything directly against you—it's simply a manifestation of their fear. Fact: If someone's offending you, fear is the driver of the offense. They are either afraid of something that will happen, losing something that they have, or getting something they don't want. If you can discover the fear that's provoking the offender, you won't be so wrapped up in being offended, and you might even find yourself in a place of empathy, compassion, and strength. You'll be able to think clearly on how to help them out of their fear, or even how *you* may have caused the fear, or both, which is the beginning of reconciliation in the relationship and a means for you to make a difference when offenses come up.

Look at people's issues discerningly today, not emotionally.

- *What is usually my first reaction when offended?*
- *What would life be like if I were rarely, if ever, offended?*

The correlation between physical motion and positive emotion should be enough to *move* you.

Today in our fast-food world of minimal physical activity, it's prudent to evaluate how our current physical condition affects our emotional state, our capacity to live life to the fullest, and the energy we have to be of value to our family, friends, and colleagues. The old adage that "the world goes to the energetic" may not be entirely true, but our gifts, talents, callings, and responsibilities fueled by a limited physicality will always get a fraction of the energy they need to be fulfilled. Add to that how lethargy, insufficient stamina, and half-energized commitment levels affect our overall mental health . . . well, upgrading our health should be a priority. Another downside of a sedentary lifestyle is decreased longevity. It is estimated that those who ignore their health shave between five and twenty-five years off their life. Add to that the incapacitating effects of illness and the burden multiplies—not just with us, but to those who must sideline their life to care for our dwindling health.

So where to start? First, realize that the effect exercise has on us is nothing short of profound. Besides the physical benefits, the mental health benefits are improved attitude, stabilized moods, and increased confidence. So start small and increase as you go. Getting the body moving with some level of consistency is a victory that creates momentum, the kind of momentum that creates a life filled with energy, clarity, and vitality.

> Consider that a little motion can have a big effect
> on emotion today ... yours and others.

- *What one thing could I do to start small? Are there other people who would join me?*
- *Have I considered how poor health is affecting my present and my future?*

Discipline is when you replace what *distracts* you with something that *impacts* you.

If ever there were a word responsible for more progress than any other, it would be the word *discipline*. The truth is, we are all experts at discipline. Some of us are disciplined at making progress, others are disciplined at staying stuck, while others are disciplined in moving backward. Assuming we desire to max out this thing called life, discipline must be understood in order to be leveraged to its full capacity.

One old-world military meaning stems from taking a branch from a tree and stripping away all that is unnecessary or useless to turn that branch into a spear—a weapon to be used for a specific purpose. It is only in the removal of that which gets in the way that the ultimate purpose of the branch is fulfilled.

Our discipline today should be no different. In today's strained economy, we'd be well served to remain clear about our objectives and goals, and strip away the endless distractions, extraneous activities, and numbing agents that pull us away from the things that will promote real progress. During healthy times, there is margin for distractions and room to entertain things that don't directly contribute to what is critical. Not today; today demands a level of discipline to make use of every moment by removing the non-essential things we comfort ourselves with. It's a posture of saying no to the small endless temptations so we can experience what we know to be important in life.

Stand guard against potential future-killers today.

- *What are the critical things I need to focus on to keep future goals on track?*
- *What distractions do I give in to?*

Patience is not to wait, but to regulate what you anticipate in a peaceful state.

If I offered you the cure for impatience, you might respond with, "I can't wait to get it."

Imagine what life would be like if you lived in a state of total patience with all people, all things, and for all time. Think about how much more fluid life would be, how much more present you would be with people, the reduced effort in which you would do things, the pace of peace you'd experience in your daily activities, and of course, the added bandwidth of thinking not wasted on impatience. Now consider all the havoc, stress, and anxiety that have occurred because you couldn't wait a little longer for things, and consider all the angst you installed into other people simply because you haven't learned to deal with your emotions. I once prayed, "God, teach me patience, but do it quickly please." Bad drivers, traffic jams, customer service hold times, etc., all had their way with my state of mind and emotion. But deep down inside, I desired to have a greater degree of control over how I held things. A close look at the day-to-day sources of my impatience revealed there was never anything I could do about any one of them. So I began to evaluate the price I was paying for my flippant emotions, and the cost was great. I not only put undue stress on myself, I added stress to anyone I was with or around, and that price was just too great. It limited my capacity and had an effect on my health, and if I lived in impatience too often, it would even shave years off my life—*physically.* Fortunately, I discovered there was always something I could invest my thought in other than investing it in impatience.

Transform the wait time into a great time today.

- *What are the common occurrences where I experience impatience?*
- *What are a few productive things I can do whenever I am forced to wait?*

The biggest conflict in helping someone with a conflict is trying to avoid any conflict.

Every one of us has a unique ability to help another in a way that nobody else can. But in today's don't-offend-anyone, don't-ruffle-any-feathers world, it's rare that someone will risk speaking boldly into a life. It's as if we value protecting our image more than we do helping people. Not surprising, but perhaps this is one reason why the world is in the condition it's in—you know, the "*me* world." If we open our eyes a few times a day, we'll see divorces coming, jobs in peril, people in addiction, and troubles mounting with those in our sphere of influence.

Odds are that no one conversation will change the course of someone's direction, but then again, any one conversation can and does. Sometimes an inquiry with a listening ear can offer real value; other times it may require you to take some conversational risks to draw out what is real. Trivial conversations dance on the surface trying to eliminate the symptoms. Effective conversations get to the root cause, and when the cause is identified, that's the beginning of growth. There's comfort in knowing that with the right heart, there is little you can do wrong when engaging in people's issues.

The fact is, we *all* need others to speak into our lives with freight-train-like conviction from time to time, and more often than not, the conversations that were painful and most challenging were the silver bullets. Some of my biggest growth moments came when a friend said enough is enough and spoke candidly with me. Those are my true friends—rare, bold, and intentional about my health and well-being. These are the lasting friendships.

If you see someone heading for a wall or a fall, don't stall ... step in with care today.

- *Am I grounded in my unique ability to serve others? Do I need to discover it?*
- *Who in my life could I engage with and make a difference? Who's in trouble?*

Matters left incomplete leave you and others feeling incomplete.

Ongoing failure to complete things can make us complete ... complete fools.

Ever wonder why we leave things incomplete? Ever consider the effects of what it means to have a bunch of undone stuff dragging behind like an emotional ball and chain wherever you go?

Although we think we can push the undone things into the backdrop of our mind, they are more front-of-mind than we think, and they weigh heavily on our presence with ourselves and with others. One look into our past and we'll likely uncover unfinished conversations, postponed reconciliations, and broken commitments in social, business, and personal circumstances that need to be dealt with. We all have at least one—some dozens, others hundreds—of fragmented, incomplete scenarios whispering, "You are in the habit of incompleteness, and so you will be incomplete." I call it "leaving a trail of brokenness behind us and a growing burden on top of us."

It's a pandemic problem defined as an unwillingness to deal with life issues in the moment, and is a means to postpone the discomfort of dealing and completing. The problem is that the postponed discomfort manifests into stress, shame, and insecurity. Unfinished business is an emotional weight we could all do without, and the weight is bigger than we think. Lifting the burden of the "undone" starts with looking into our "incomplete files" and cleaning up old messes; meeting with those left on the trail of brokenness to get real, deal, and heal. There is irreplaceable value when we go on a journey of restoration. Life has a way of honoring every step, every word, and every meeting when we go down the road of completing things. Not only will our relationship with others be strengthened, the way in which we value ourselves and others will improve as well.

**Complete whatever is incomplete
so you can feel more complete today.**

- *Am I in the habit of leaving things or issues unfinished?*
- *What one thing if completed would take some weight off my shoulders?*

To stay grounded in life, we should take a leap of faith every day.

There's always a chance of loss with risk. You could lose trepidation, stagnancy, and fear.

Every day presents itself with an opportunity to risk into serious growth and personal development. Tasks, meetings, conversations, and initiatives are all the playgrounds of risk. I know you might be saying, "Oh, not another ShiftPoint on risk." Well, consider that I am now taking a risk that the last ShiftPoint on risk *may* have only sunk in to a level. So for me, I will risk being redundant, looking like a fool, or being wrong because I care about people, their growth, and their transformation. I also know that we retain only about 10 percent of what we read, and repetition of good things is a great thing . . . an essential thing. Not to mention, few things in life make us feel more alive and vibrant than being in the midst of a good risk. Pushing the envelope of ourselves has a crazy way of making us feel totally out of control and yet completely in control and resolved at the same time. It puts us in the zone, where no matter what the outcome, the risk will provide additions to our life toolbox that we cannot acquire any other way. Our foundation, solidarity, and life momentum all get stronger with every stretch. I call it "slipping on a banana peel . . . *forward*." Søren Kierkegaard confirms it: "To dare is to lose one's footing momentarily. To not dare is to lose oneself." Risking is a no-lose proposition: When we risk and succeed, we benefit, as do others in our life, and we become an inspiration for them to do the same. When we risk and fail, we grow wiser, more aware, and move through life on a more solid foundation with every step.

You know where you need to risk;
think it through and risk forward.

• Do I find there is any real growth in avoiding risk and playing it safe?

• *What one risk would give my life more vitality and purpose?*

Days are long, life is short. Go figure!

Would it be wise to take some time . . . to think about time? Well . . . it's about time.

Time is an interesting thing. The speed at which time travels never changes, and constant with every clock in the world, a second is a second, an hour is an hour, and a day is a day. Time never stops. There are no pause buttons.

Even a broken clock gets older—its hands are still but time ticks on. Now consider a clock that counts down from, let's say, 12 million minutes. That would be about the time I have left, assuming I live to about eighty and I'm now approaching fifty. No matter how I slice time, one fact remains about this uninterruptable blessing we have been given: The value of time is not measured by time itself, nor by our perception of it; it is measured by how we participate in the time we've been given, and the way in which we leverage every moment, hour, day, and year. We have been given great capacity to be stewards of our time. We can have a major influence in the way we live out our dreams, make an impact in the world, and give of ourselves. We all have the same unique ability to increase the value of moments by our commitment to maximize each of them. Or we can sedate ourselves with the illusion that there is an endless supply of time and live with no drive to capitalize on the most incredible gift of all. Through time, it has been shown that a day may take place in an effective hour and an hour in a productive minute. Yet time is black and white, nothing gray; that which is lost may never be regained. It would be of value to spend some time thinking about your time.

Consider the time that is left on *your* clock today.

- *Am I in the habit of maximizing time, or do I not give it much thought?*
- *What do I want to get out of the minutes to decades ahead?*

If someone else talked to us the way we often talk to ourselves, we'd slap them.

I'm bad; I can't do it; they won't like me; it's going to end in disaster; I'm going to fail." And on and on.

Among the most impactful conversations we can have are the ones we have with ourselves. They influence every area of our life . . . powerfully! Careful attention should be paid here, as the quantity of conversations we have with ourselves every day outweighs the conversations we have with others no less than several hundred to one.

The impact of these internal conversations that are woven throughout our day-to-day activities can really interfere with our life. The little voice inside our head is jabbering away 24/7. But the question is: "Is the little voice encouraging or discouraging, creating fear or confidence, peace or anxiety, focus or distraction?" Spending quiet time to evaluate the conversations you have with yourself is a great exercise, but do this in real time where thoughts are current and fresh and you can study the details of how you think. Given a serious commitment to reengineer the conversations we have with ourselves, life could be radically more rewarding and predictable if we stopped the flow of uncontrolled, undisciplined internal conversations.

The mind needs exercise to change the way it works for you. And minds left alone to fly on autopilot will eventually run out of fuel and crash. We could all stand to spend a little time reengineering the way we talk to ourselves so every thought builds up in contrast to tearing down. At least we should tell ourselves that!

> **Change the way you talk to yourself today.**
> **The return is astounding.**

- *Are the conversations I have with myself inhibiting or motivating?*
- *Is my instinct to control my thought life or to casually let my mind run free?*

The world needs more humor so badly, it's laughable!

Last time I checked, I still had my funny bone.

The world we live in seems to be getting more serious every day. The state of world affairs, the economy, global business equalization, and changes in technology are moving at an alarming rate, and the intensity is seeping through the media straight into our lives. The tone of society has flattened to a survive-instead-of-thrive mentality, and the focus is on intensity rather than on levity. Humor these days seems to be relegated to sitcoms and stand-up comedians, most of which rank high on the cliché scale, or are simply just rank and not very funny. But where is "true" humor today? Believe it or not, there's a little bit of "funny" in just about everyone. And although we may never make it to stand-up comic status or star in a sitcom, we each have the capacity to contribute humor in our own unique way, to bring a bit of healing laughter into a world that is taking life too darn seriously. But not everyone is a comic. For example, I can't tell jokes very well, but I can be witty at times. In fact, one out of every three attempts gets a real strong response. I just have to pay the price of the two misses, as do others. The truth is, the one win is worth it, and I believe the other two aren't as bad as I make them out to be. People appreciate it when you try and are humored by failure or success in your attempts. In fact, sometimes the failure is funnier than the success.

- *Might it be fun to work on my own unique brand of humor?*
- *Will I be willing to risk looking foolish to bring a little levity to others?*

Bad listeners hear themselves. Average listeners hear the words. Good listeners hear the issues. Great listeners hear the heart.

Do you listen on autopilot, or with intentionality, purpose, and focus? The skill of intentional listening is among the most valuable assets we can possess. Like breathing is to the body, listening is to relationships, learning, and growth. Stop listening and things wither and die. Our attentiveness to others is a catalyst that breathes success into business and social interaction, but quality listening is always in jeopardy due to urgency, distractions, and its number one adversary—multitasking in conversations. Being partially in a conversation and partially elsewhere adds up to a complete relational disconnect. In fact, anything less than total focus in conversation is the beginning of the end of that relationship. People get it when we're tentatively listening, no matter how we try to disguise it.

So rather than listening on the surface, our commitment to hear past any static and straight into the heart of individuals is a social grace that will bring intense richness to relationships. And those we talk to have a way of becoming conversationally brilliant when we listen to their words and their heart. Attending in this rare and caring manner is practiced by few, as it demands focus and an all-out assault on *autopilot* or *casual* listening. But the rewards of doing so are nothing short of extraordinary. Listening with intentionality draws out the best in people and makes way for lasting relationships that create amazing results. To block out all distractions and listen beyond the words is to build trust and intimacy, and it will position you as a friend and leader to everyone you meet.

Stay attuned to the heart of people today, and watch them become alive, attentive, and fascinating.

- *Do I attempt to listen to the heart in conversations or just the words?*
- *Do I bring meaning into conversations or simply try to get through them?*

Change is a discipline, not a daydream.

On your mark, get set . . . CONTEMPLATE! Just doesn't sound right, does it?

The thought of change is an attractive proposition for humans. One might even say we're addicted to change. Even people whom we see as stuck are changing by becoming more stuck as time goes on. Change never stops, and we are all born to be in a continual state of transformation. Regardless, we have a love/hate relationship with change. Although we love the idea of change through the improvements it provides, we're not always attracted to the work that precedes it. In fact, rather than investing thought into what transformation will take, we often use the same mental energy to fantasize rather than plan for change. The deception is that thinking about change will create motivation when, in fact, thinking about it tends to demotivate, derail, and in some cases destroy the possibility before it even starts. I've always believed that lasting inspiration and motivation come just after starting the process of changing something rather than at the beginning. It's when we experience small doses of growth and see results that change develops the momentum needed to leap over obstacles and break down walls. Thinking doesn't do that. Aside from the rare times when life gifts a change of heart, mind, or circumstance, most of the time we are the catalysts to create the change we need in our life.

Change the way you change today.

• *Do I spend more time thinking about change or actually changing?*
• *What things could I change this day, week, month, or year?*

Married couples, please note: If you make a note to write a note, your spouse will certainly take note.

My marriage would be better if I wrote a love note every now and then." Duly noted.

Speaking of notes, you might want to take note of a rare but significant reality: Marriages are headed in one of two directions—toward intimacy or toward divorce. If couples are headed down the middle, they are likely moving down the difficult path of separation or divorce. Status quo does not work in marriage. Harsh as that may sound, the divorce rate proves I'm at least 51 percent accurate. Another 25 percent of marriages are just surviving, another 15 percent are doing OK, and only a small percentage are thriving. This small percentage is thriving because they know that marriage is a living entity that is kept alive and well by breathing new life into it every day. They also know that letting the relationship go and thinking it will somehow stay together without putting forth the effort is not only ridiculous, it's the beginning of the end.

Call me ignorant, but I believe all relationships are held together by small gestures of love, kindness, and fun, not the occasional big gesture. I'm also convinced that if every married couple left an occasional note sharing a little something special about the other, we'd make a small dent in the national divorce rate. It can be a thank-you, encouragement, apology, poem . . . whatever. It is a symbol of commitment to value each other, and for whatever reason, notes have an amazing ability to always come at the perfect time, no matter what time it is.

Make a note to share more kind thoughts in your pad.

- *When was the last time I wrote a little note to my spouse?*
- *Will I set digital or old-school reminders and make a note to share a note?*

Whoever says "You can't change the world" . . . rarely does!

E very day we deliver a presence into the world. We rarely think about it on a macroscale like that. But what if one day everyone on the planet were to wake up and max out their capacity to love, care, serve, and encourage everyone they contacted and provided an attitude that enrolled others to sustain that the following day. The world would be changed . . . in a day!

I'm sure we'd all agree that society as a whole could benefit from an attitude adjustment or even a complete overhaul in how it views the gift of life. But in today's world of economic challenges, global transformation, and political uncertainties, pessimism seems to be winning the battle over optimism—word by word, belief by belief, action by action. It seems that with every turn we are barraged with strategically packaged hopelessness coming from all sources. At the end of the day, however, it is our commitment to manage our own attitudes and actions that will make an impact with those in our centers of influence.

Today, like every day, you'll have several opportunities to impact someone's life in a meaningful and powerful way. An encouraging word, an act of kindness, even a quick prayer for someone may not be considered grandiose enough to change *the* world, but rest assured, it will change *their* world. That in itself, in its own seemingly small way, makes the world a better place. It all starts with changing the internal conversation that "I can change the world; I will change the world," and ignoring the rhetoric of the skeptic, pessimist, and doomsayer.

Use your attitude, talents, and abilities to impact someone's world today.

- *Whose world can I be a part of improving today?*
- *Am I so wrapped up in my world that I miss improving others' worlds?*

In a conflict, being aware of how others will receive the statements you make will make a powerful statement.

If common sense makes for progress, common sensitivity will do that and more!

In the heat of anger, words can actually do more damage than physical abuse. A bruise can go away, but certain words can be indelibly inscribed on the heart for a lifetime. As strange as it seems, I can remember things that were said to me more than any physical trauma I've experienced in my life by a long shot. They shaped my thoughts about life, and I've been contending with some of them for quite a long time.

Our words have life-altering power and can be just as damaging as they can be healing, so we need to govern our words with the sensitivity they require. I'll admit, searching for the best way to say something in the thick of it can be a little work; not considering what we say can result in much more work and irreparable harm. And when we backtrack after saying something harmful ("I didn't really mean that"), we're simply adding insult to injury. People know better.

Although most don't like the word *restraint* very much, it is a viable discipline to practice in business and social conversations . . . especially in conflict. The discipline of not letting our words get past either our thinking or our reason works wonders; we use fewer words, convey more meaning, and get better results. People appreciate it when we've thought about how to say something to them. It's a reminder for them to do the same, and it creates a mutual respect that makes every conversation more peaceful, productive, and rewarding.

Make a statement by holding back harmful statements today.

- *When in conflict, does my anger control my words or do I?*
- *Do I need to ask forgiveness of anyone whom I have hurt with my words?*

Sometimes I'm so visionless in life, I need sleep just to avoid the pain of my complacency.

If we go to bed and we keep our eyes closed too long, our life-vision will stay in the dark as well.

We go to great lengths in life to avoid pain. One of those ways is found in how much we want to sleep or even need to sleep. How much do we *actually* need? The answer might be less than we think. And how much we *want* may be related to how intentional we are about our life and the vision we have . . . or don't have. Some indications are that when we are living in our purpose or are impassioned by a vision and working toward its fulfillment, the desire to sleep reduces, productivity increases, and the body adjusts to the right amount of sleep rather than oversleeping. The excitement of life and working on a future worth having can drive how much sleep we want or need into perspective. It can make extending daylight hours a thrill, and sleep becomes a healthy need instead of an emotional crutch. And then there's quality of sleep to consider. Through personal experience, I've discovered that sleep when living out my vision is generally better than when I'm complacent, and my need for extra rest is minimized. The starting point for everything we do is vision. It is the thing that pulls us out of discomfort, drives us to stay motivated, and helps us maneuver through obstacles. Not to mention, it gets us out of bed a little bit earlier and makes the need or desire to sleep during the day a thing of the past. If our desire is to minimize the pain and maximize the value of the time we've been given here on earth, complacency isn't a good strategy, nor is sleep ever going to make the dreams you have come true.

Activate your vision for a more restful, peaceful, and fulfilling life today.

- *Do I have a vision that wakes me up every day or one that drives me to sleep?*
- *Will I get up a little earlier tomorrow and spend some time thinking about this?*

Fear doesn't go away.
I'm *afraid* it's true.

Fear manifests in percentages, from just a tinge of fear to sheer terror. Some of our fears are circumstantial due to events and happenings, and other fears build up slowly over time into a subtle to severe undertone in our life that winds up in our way of being. But fear really doesn't come from an event, occurrence, or situation; it comes alive through our perspective of these things, the way we choose to hold them.

For every fear, there is a way of relating to the fear that will minimize, even vaporize it. Through a small investment of thinking through the fear, like working with a lump of clay, you begin to form something new, the way you'd like to see it, hold it, and feel it. The challenge? The next fear is on the way.

The key to managing fear is pretty simple, like managing debt. Don't let fears pile up. Ignoring the fears and not working with them is not a strategy to manage fear into a healthy state—healthy, meaning learn to think about what's possible and process the fears proactively instead of reactively. Ignoring the fears only prolongs the inevitable of having to deal with them at some point. So the question becomes, why not deal with fears in the present before they build into chronic anxiety, nervous breakdowns, depression . . . even heart attacks. Take serious issue with every fear as a relentless enemy, one with a clear goal of limiting your potential and your happiness. Invest in deep contemplation, and when fear rears its head, seek counsel from others and acquire knowledge from sources to help free your mind from past or present fears. Stay disciplined in this and you'll discover a repeatable strategy that works to manage fears . . . so they don't manage you.

Spend some time thinking through your fears today.

- *Should I place more focus on removing fear from my life?*
- *What price am I paying by ignoring fears, thinking they will just go away?*

Add-*vice*

Sometimes the best advice you can give is the advice you don't give. There's a reason why so many jokes and musings are centered around advice. Most advice is a joke and quite amusing. And yet there's no shortage of advice floating around out there. In fact, there's some coming to a conversation near you. The truth is, most people love to give advice, and yet most people don't take it. There's a reason for that. When we give advice to others, what we're really giving is a potential "vice" in the form of dependency and ignoring the opportunity for the other to research on their own terms, through their own lens and experience. The art and science of helping someone in challenging circumstances is not about telling them what to do. We rarely have all the facts, background, or insight to do that well anyway, not to mention life is seldom a formula, nor are there prepackaged answers we can count on.

If we want to be of value to other people, helping them from A to B is best achieved through inquiry rather than toying with half-educated statements based on our own experiences. And it shouldn't be light inquiry either. It should be so thorough that by the time the other has answered all the right questions, they'll have given themselves the advice they need. Moving others to think through things on their own facilitates their clarifying the issue, not you. And once they think it through and choose their own way, it creates the best chance of action and lasting impact. Think questions like, "Have you considered? . . . What would it be like if? . . . What would a person like that do?" Think communication, not dictation; think investigation, not experimentation. It's the best for all, and that's my advice.

Don't add vice . . . add value to others today.

- *Do I have all the facts before I give others my feedback?*
- *How do I feel when someone gives me advice without knowing all the details?*

Reflect, and then connect!

Make sure to put a net in your networking . . . a safety net.

It's safe to say that we all have benefited from networking. It's also safe to say that we've made some bad connections in the past and maintain the potential of it happening again. But if we realized how much of our credibility was at stake when we facilitate the connection of business relationships, we would reflect deeply . . . not connect loosely.

There are many variables to consider when referring, including the reality of mutual value, probability percentage of relationship, potential conflicts, even personality styles. A little thinking goes a long way to facilitating quality referrals, as will open, honest, and detailed conversations with both referrals in advance. Asking specific questions and sharing the fullness of what's real with both parties is essential to creating a solid fit and determining if there are any obstacles in the way of a relationship being formed. The more specific and detailed you are in the conversation, the better both parties will feel about the meeting, and there will be fewer surprises. It serves the referrals well when we qualify connections with intentionality, and it reflects positively on our reputation when we do our homework. Truth be told, referrals should be so well teed up that success will be imminent upon meeting. The nice part of making great connections with people is the reciprocation of tight referrals, the enhancement of our reputation, and the certainty of knowing we added value to those we trust and care about.

- *When facilitating a referral, do I reveal the details or just the generalities?*
- *How do I feel when someone gives me a referral or two that go nowhere?*

Speak from a pure heart, and what you say will undoubtedly speak for itself.

Whenever you speak to a group, leave your head at home and speak from the heart.

Ever go watch someone speak, only to leave underwhelmed, underinspired, and that feeling perhaps you overpaid . . . even if the event was free? Me too, and all too often! The reason for this is basic. Most talks are people just saying words, focusing on giving the appropriate hand gestures, making the right amount of eye contact, walking to the left and to the right, and delivering on Speech 101.

In today's world, manufactured eloquence and practiced polish in public speaking is dying slowly, as is data regurgitation and slick delivery. People aren't necessarily moved by what we say or how well we say it but by our conviction when we're sharing. It's about the authenticity of our heart and how much we truly care for the audience that sits before us.

Transformational communicators are those who are clear about what they are committed to cause in the hearts and minds of their audience . . . specifically. They stand for transformation, believing that their heart will do a great work regardless of the evaluation sheet or whatever the infamous voice inside their head has to say. Their commitment to facilitate growth with their audience drives their focus away from themselves to those who have committed their precious time to come, to learn, and to grow.

The net effect? The speaker and their nerves reduce to an appropriate size, authenticity shows up loud and clear, lives are radically touched and transformed, walls are torn down, and value gets delivered to everyone, including the speaker.

Next time you speak, replace your technique with an urgency to cause a revolution.

- *When I speak, is my focus on me, my audience, or the evaluation sheet?*
- *Am I more about delivering data or causing transformation with my audience?*

Get to know the point of "know" return.

Imagine a world where every goal set forth was realized. Now imagine *that* economy. Looks a little different than the one we're in, doesn't it? The battlefield of goals leaves many casualties. Perhaps one out of ten actually make it to maturity, if that. So many goals, so few met.

One of the reasons goals are unmet and dreams aren't realized is because they often don't get to that critical point—the point of where you clearly know there will be an actual return on your efforts, or the point where turning back doesn't make sense. Typically, people will start goals with ample enthusiasm only to lose motivation because the evidence of the initiative hasn't arrived yet. As a result of there being "no visible return," shortsightedness sets in, the commitment languishes, and things die off only to happen again and again.

The crazy thing is the goal never gets hurt, as it has no feelings. When goals are abandoned, it is we who pay the price. Our confidence suffers, our resources dwindle, and our emotions and reputation take the hit, while the goal sits there and says, "Hey pal, I'm still here, you can come back, I'll take you back, let's go again." Goals are designed to help us, not hurt us; further us, not stop us; and make us feel a sense of accomplishment, not hopelessness.

The point of "know return," however, requires tenacity to get there. It's nothing more than simply "going again." It's a stay-focused, stay-committed mind-set that has returns showing up all over the place, including in our spirit. Bottom line? In order for the value to show up, comfort and convenience have to be sidelined until the returns hit that critical point. Otherwise, what's the point?

Start the journey to the point of "know" return today.

- Will I take five minutes to list out my unfinished goal pile . . . or mountain?
- Is the return on one of my goals just a little more tenacity away?

The only way to lose an argument is not to learn from it.

Arguments are a wonderful thing, if we're willing to look at our part in them.

When I first got married and my wife and I would get into an argument, my first inclination was to steer blame away from myself. I prided myself in debate, but what I was winning was emptiness, strife, and discontentment. My default was to always protect myself from being wrong, but what I was protecting was my arrogance, self-righteousness, and pride, all because I wanted to be right, and I was. Dead right—dead to peace, dead to learning, and dead to possibilities in having a better, more consistent relationship.

After a year or so of this lunacy, I decided that there must be a better way to handle arguments. After a bit of contemplation, a new paradigm emerged that directed me to consider the following: that when problems developed with my wife and me, I should instinctively look first to myself and examine how I may have contributed to the problem. This was my new default and where I would go at the first sign of an argument. Inevitably, I would find something in my way of being, my actions, my communication, or my lack of actions that contributed to, if not caused, the conflict. Whether minute or substantial, if I confessed my part, it would bring hope, trust, and workability to the situation in a matter of seconds. Any other disposition would usually take days and sometimes longer to work out, all because I wanted to skirt a few minutes of accounting for my part in the breakdown.

Account for your role in things today.

- *What is my normal response when an argument arises?*
- *What would arguments be like if I sought to learn how to better value the other person?*

Persistence is that one little word that made everything ever thought of become that which is today.

Persistence vs. intelligence. Without persistence, intelligence isn't very smart!

Ask any accomplished individual about what it took to be successful, and you won't hear, "Well, I started, then I stopped, then I waited, then I dabbled, then I started something new, and then I repeated the cycle." What you'll hear is something like, "I don't know, I just kept focused on the task, didn't get distracted, and amazingly things fell into place and the right people came along. It's really that simple." And it is. Most people think there is something special about those who have become successful. Words like *intelligent*, *well-connected*, *thought leader*, *charismatic*, and more are used to describe them. And although some of those may be true, they would all be meaningless if they weren't girded in persistence and tenacity. Persistence is typically the only ingredient that is needed above all else for any accomplishment, and certainly nothing happens without it. So it goes without saying that there's something to be said about staying the course. Even if the goal isn't the right one, the process of staying in the game not only makes things clearer in life, it brings us to life. It's that "persistence motivation" that drives agendas and in the process builds our character, confidence, and a list of progressive adjectives. On the flip side, if the goal is the right one, persistence makes success imminent, and you get the improved character, confidence, and a list of progressive adjectives that go along with it.

Don't even think of quitting today.

- *How do distractions, starts, and stops affect my goals?*
- *Where would it make sense to test an unwavering commitment to persistence?*

Don't be a blockhead with time. Use your head and block out time!

Isn't it about time to get control of your time? Time is always in short supply. When we're young, there's never enough time to do our homework; when we're adults there's never enough time to take care of the house, get our kids to do their homework, do our work, and do all the other things that need to get done. Even when people retire, they claim they are busier during retirement than when they were working. Safe to say we all view time the same way—there's never enough of it to do what needs to get done or what we want to do. Welcome to reality.

Life's biggest opportunity will never be how we view time but how much we extract from the time we have been given. Like squeezing juice from an orange, we have the capacity to get a great deal more out of the minutes, hours, and days we have if we proactively make a commitment to do so. Whether it's leveraging our time to improve our knowledge in our career, spending more time with the family, getting in shape, losing some weight, writing a book, starting a hobby, or whatever floats the boat, there will never be enough time to do it unless we develop the amazingly productive habit of time-blocking. It is truly the only way to challenge the reality of time and, in theory, to slow the clock down and squeeze what you want out of life.

The process is pretty simple. Regardless of whether you use a hard copy, mobile phone, or tablet calendar, the method is to start the elusive habit of blocking out time. That's the easy part. The secret sauce is actually doing what is scheduled as if your life depended on it and allowing the accomplishment of that time to create the motivation needed for a lasting commitment. Motivation, by the way, is not needed to get things done; time-blocking and commitment are the life-giving combination to activating all things.

Schedule it, do it, and watch things get done.

- *Do I have an adequate scheduling tool to time-block?*
- *What would I like to start working on? What needs more time committed to it?*

Before every meeting or event, if you want to minimize your nerves . . . then maintain a heart to serve.

One sure way to serve our nerves is to have the verve to serve.

Now that you've been on the planet for a while, you've probably noticed the unpredictable nature of nerves and would probably pay handsomely for a remedy to either control or remove these raw and intense feelings from your life. Going into an important meeting or event can shift our nerves into "overstrive" and rob all the peace, joy, and effectiveness from the experience. The more important the event, the more apparent our nerves become. Sometimes nerves become so "in our face" that they threaten to sabotage the entire outcome—and they can, depending on where we place our focus.

A quick evaluation of these edgy feelings will reveal that our nervousness exists because our attention is on what we'll do wrong, what we will miss, or what we won't get—all issues of self. But, almost miraculously, when our focus is on others and serving them, the most intense nerves will become manageable, if not disappear altogether. In fact, this selfless heart-set will usher in feelings of peace and confidence that will make every event a home run. It's all but fact that serving and nerves rarely exist in the same space.

Connect intently to the serve today and watch the nerves go away!

- When going into meetings, is my focus on me and what might go wrong?
- In meetings, what value would focusing on others and their needs bear?

Vengeance is mine,
sayeth the bored.

Paybacks: No matter how they go, why is it we're the ones who pay a price?

Within a world of diversities, blended cultures, and all walks of life in all states of mind, it's easy to accept that we will be offended by others' behaviors or their differences hundreds if not thousands of times before we leave this world. The idea that we will somehow be able to avoid others' tromping on our emotional, mental, or physical turf is simply unrealistic. In fact, if we get through a day or two without someone rubbing us the wrong way, consider it a flat-out miracle. Life is complex enough without investing valuable time, energy, and resources into the ridiculous sport of offense reciprocation. It's the bored and the visionless who plan to make offenders pay in some subtle or perhaps serious way. Conversely, those with vision and purpose don't have time for vengeance, as they value their time and precious mental and emotional resources, and they govern their feelings by not letting others have ownership of them. Those of real character will more often than not use their strength to seek reconciliation rather than revenge and perhaps scrutinize how they may have contributed to the offense in the first place. Offenses are a two-way street 95 percent of the time, and as for vindictiveness . . . a dead-end street, perhaps literally!

**You have better things to focus
on than being offended today.**

- *Would it be better to control my emotions or risk losing everything?*
- *Who am I making pay, or planning to make pay, for something they did?*

Skill is a great thing.
Relevancy is great progress!

Differentiation is meaningless without relevancy.

In the world of branding, it used to be that being different was the big to-do. The differentiation movement, they called it. "Differentiate or die!" they screamed. Well, that worked fine when there was a big disparity between one thing and the next, one product and the other, and one person and the other. Today, all things are of pretty decent quality, no matter what country they are from, and most people are pretty good at what they do because competition has demanded that we rise to a certain level of play or get fired from the team. In today's world of available information and training, we all have skills—some rough, some refined, some off the charts. But the achievement of goals, visions, and dreams only happens when our skills, whether natural or learned, meet relevance. As mentioned, with brands there has often been an emphasis on skills needing to be unique in order to be compelling and impactful. Not that differentiation is dead, but relevance gives life to differentiation. It is the foundation of it, and without relevance, differentiation is odd, awkward, and out of place. The key to becoming relevant is to be on a constant journey of discovering what is important to those we desire to be relevant to, then building our brand, our offerings, and our way of being to fulfill those needs, wants, and demands tangibly and consistently. Relevance is the one attribute that ensures we will be of specific value to those in our personal and business lives, and is the assurance of our success, influence, and even our contentment.

Evaluate your skills and check relevancy to your audiences today.

- *Am I focused on being more different or more relevant?*
- *Have I inquired about my relevancy in personal and business relationships?*

When qualifying others for anything, you can foretell the future. It's called a solid reference check.

Past performance is the foresight needed to predict future performance.

Teaming, befriending, or hiring someone who is a bad fit can be an emotional, financial, and relational catastrophe. The repercussions are endless, and yet people are hired, enrolled, and invited into critical functions and relationships every day with little or no due diligence. The reason? Reference checks take time and effort to do them right. It's a journey of discovery to find out the details of times past, and it requires breaking the habit of shooting from the hip and instead taking a slower, sniper-like approach where a single shot nails it. It's not only beneficial for us to get this right, it's also a stewardship issue to put people in positions they belong in vs. positions they think they can do. For business or personal functions, the time it takes to do a comprehensive check on references is nothing compared to the loss of time and money associated with advertising, training, and cultural acclimation, only to do it over again because it wasn't the right fit. Whether hiring for a nanny, employee, vendor, or kitchen contractor, Google "effective reference checks," extract the questions, and create your own method. Skill set, dependability, and track record are the basics, but real reference checks include temperament, willingness to serve, how one deals with intensity, conflict, breakdowns, and other personality traits that are not addressed in Reference Check 101, nor do they show up on the résumé.

P.S. It would be wise to check references and opinions on *everyone* you'll be in relationship with—*casual* or *serious.*

Dig a little deeper today so you're not digging
yourself out of a mess tomorrow.

- How has not checking references caused a loss of productivity, even sanity?
- What next hire, affiliation, or relationship could benefit from a reference check?

If how you multiply *divides*, it will simply add to your *subtraction*.

If how we grow reduces those around us, then it is we who are getting smaller.

If you look at how things grow in nature, you'll see there are many things that have to become temporarily damaged or die off to make way for new growth. This is not the case with us humans. Things don't *have* to become a mess for a period of time, nor do our main physical components have to die for us to grow and develop.

Truth is, we were born to grow, to multiply, and to expand beyond the borders of what we think is possible. What we are not born to do is leave a trail of collateral damage and dead relationships behind as we grow—a common occurrence for serial entrepreneurs, those feverishly climbing the corporate ladder, or those who are bent on living their passions to the fullest. For us to grow, we require people to be in the mix with us, and how we treat those people will impact our overall fulfillment, not just the accomplishment of what is at hand. If co-workers, partners, alliances, and friends in your life are nothing more than a means to your end, it will divide and subtract in the long run. If your family gets sidelined because your commitment to grow supersedes your commitment to your family, it will divide and subtract. If your friends become a conduit to get what you want, whereby you find yourself tempted to leverage every friendship for your growth, it will divide and subtract.

Work/life balance—you've heard the phrase before, and perhaps you're thinking it will slow growth, and it does . . . by a small percentage, but not nearly as much as being fired, having a heart attack, getting divorced, or mending broken relationships.

Add to others as you multiply yourself today.

- *Does my growth consider the growth of others growing along with me?*
- *Are people in my life just a means to an end?*

The remedy for emotional pain is found in our perspectives of it.

Our view of pain will determine how badly pain hurts.

As humans, we go through a great deal of pain to avoid pain rather than accepting it as part of our day-to-day experience. But pain is that part of life that, when embraced and dealt with appropriately, will reveal such incredible value that it can be almost pleasurable. It can become so valuable that you hold pain as an ally, a friend who delivers the gift long after the birthday, so to speak. Unfortunately, one of the things they don't prepare you for in universities, educational programs, and motivational trainings is the reality and beauty of pain. Somehow in the midst of all that curriculum, the one thing that is guaranteed to show up in our lives in great abundance is not only *not* addressed, it's feared as a discussion point, perhaps because it's too painful a topic. As a result, when pain hits, and it always does, there's a feeling of shock, followed by anguish, followed by hopelessness, and eventually a loss—a loss of momentum and the vision of what could be next—all because our training and our instinct have indicated that pain is not supposed to be here and we should avoid it at all costs. If you can get your head and heart around the idea that pain doesn't hurt, it helps, that it's not a bad thing but a learning thing, that it's not a limitation but an opportunity, then pain will be fuel, not fire, to your life and to your growth. And when it shows up, you'll simply say, "Bring it on," then move on.

Realize the purpose in pain. Let it drive you,
teach you, and inspire you today.

- *Do I repel pain when it shows up, or do I search for the value in it?*
- *Is the price I'm paying to avoid pain causing more pain than the pain itself?*

Those who go to great lengths acquire great strengths.

It's the extra that creates the extraordinary.

It's no surprise that whenever we practice something we desire to do in life, we get better. Some get better quickly, and for others it takes time. But one fact remains—practice doesn't make perfect, it just makes better. Just a dose of reality, as perfect is indefinable in the natural sense and is subject to the opinion of those who are . . . well, "imperfect." Another dose of reality is that in those areas of life we are passionate about, we have the ability to strengthen our capacity, but we also have the strange ability to live in the fantasy that things will strengthen on their own, or that a little effort goes a long way. It doesn't. Not today, not tomorrow . . . not anymore. In fact, in today's competitive world, the only thing more apparent than the need to be on our A-game is the reality that we either *improve* or get *replaced*, we go *beyond* or get left *behind*. Unfortunately, living a life of doing just enough to get by can have one stuck in just that—just getting by. Contrarily, going *beyond* what is expected in all areas of our life, although a bit more work, can form a habit that actually makes life easier, not harder, more rewarding, less stressful, and more enjoyable at every turn. The value for yourself and others when you go beyond expectations is worth the stretch, and in the process, you'll strengthen your character, confidence, and conviction while being an inspiration to those around you.

Avoid being neglected. Go beyond what is expected today.

- *Am I stuck in the rut of doing just enough to get by?*
- *What would things be like if I did everything a little better than expected?*

Shatter life's rearview mirror.

There's really no future in blaming your past for your present.

As mentioned earlier, by the time we reach age four, some experts say our past (the whole four years of our past) will largely determine how we live out the rest of our lives. The formative years they call them, and it would be wise to note it is modern psychology that leans on this position. Although there's some truth in this notion, it is far from law and shouldn't be held as such, nor should any other indicator that our past will determine our future. For many adults who are not content with their lives, most current excuses are used up or overused, and the only workable one left is that the past is the reason why the present and future can't be all they are intended to be. The weight of "whatever once was" has conveniently become the back door to avoid bold moves in life, and we give power to something that no longer exists. Life gets put on hold, and as a result we end up living in the grave of our past, a dead zone where the only possibility that exists to get us out of it is to let it go and leave it behind.

To live in the fullness of what life has for us is not a fear-free, risk-free zone. It appears safer at times to use the past as an excuse to avoid uncharted new territory because we lose the certainty to look good, feel good, be right, and be in control—all illusions, all insufficient for any lasting gratification. If we want to maximize our life, it would be best if we ran the race to win, despite our past. I doubt that many victories would be had if we looked in life's rearview mirror throughout the race.

Focus on what's ahead and leave the past behind today!

- *Am I giving too much credence to my past determining my future?*
- *What beliefs were formed in my past that I'd rather leave behind?*

You know you have influence when even your absence has a presence.

Is love more powerful than influence? What is love, then, without influence?

Imagine having unlimited influence with others. What would it be like having 100 percent buy-in to everything you said? Kings, priests, politicians, and moguls all knocking on your door to follow your counsel, move the way you said to move, open their wallets to buy what you were selling, and follow your lead. And then you woke up! Influence is among the most powerful attributes that exist when it comes to getting things done. Actually, I haven't met a person yet who would not like to have more influence with others. If I *did* meet such a person, I'm not sure how exciting the experience would be.

Sales professionals, parents, kids, pastors, athletes, leaders, businesspeople—virtually everyone can benefit from having more influence with others. The bad news is you can't buy positive influence, not unless you're unscrupulous and have means. Regardless, there's a more predictable way to gain influence with those around you, and that is to make it a mission to be in the business of creating value for other people. By value, I mean discovering what will make people's lives better, easier, more productive, and more rewarding, and will deliver that which will improve these areas. This is the engine of influence, and the horsepower therein is unlimited. Do this one simple thing—add value, and not only will your influence with those around you become strong enough to achieve anything; even your absence, whether during this life or when you leave it, will have a lasting impact with others. That is influence.

Make it a mission to make a notable difference in others' lives today.

- *Might I benefit from an influence check in business, family, or community?*
- *Where can I create more value for others to create more influence?*

Other people don't own your emotions—you do.

Who controls how you feel, what you let in, and the state of your mind?

Wouldn't it be nice to have the ability to be confident when you want, to right-size your feelings into a manageable state when you need to, and to reduce stress at will? Feel impossible? Well, it's only a feeling, and even though it may *feel* impossible, owning your emotions begins by acknowledging who maintains the keys to drive how you feel. If you give others the keys to your emotions, which they have zero right to have, then you hand over your feelings for others to play with at will. Unfortunately, no one is ever going to care for your emotions the way you can, and the beginning point of emotional control starts first in the mind.

The idea of investing in thoughts and working things through before they turn to emotion means we must hold the thought captive for a few moments before it manifests. In fact, the word *captive*, in its root meaning, comes from keeping something from moving by controlling it with the tip of a spear. Liken that to the thoughts we think, and you can see there is a process to controlling our emotions, instead of emoting our way through life. The undisciplined process of feel first, deal second, and contend with the chaos third can be replaced with think first, process second, feel what I want to feel third. Minute by minute, we have a great opportunity to practice the art of self-control through quick bits of contemplation all the way to small, detailed meditations in all our situations. Each circumstance of your life is an opportunity to learn how to contend with every thought and bring greater control to every emotion; otherwise those same circumstances will rule over you.

What would it feel like to gain more control over how I feel today?

- *Where in my life do I let others control how I feel?*
- *Am I willing to hold thoughts captive for more control over my emotions?*

If someone treats you like a number, get *their* number.

You can change the mood of someone in the blink of a try.

I'm sure you've noticed that the way people treat you can sometimes be hostile, demeaning, demanding, detached, or patronizing. But is there a way to eliminate such behavior?

Mastering the ability to shift others' moods begins by considering that no matter how poorly someone treats us, there is always a way to draw out the beauty that is in them. I've come to discover that there is always beauty under the ugly—if we can get *their number* in the midst of them trying to get *ours*. Rather than getting wrapped up in someone's temporary or ongoing dysfunction, we can engage with their toxicity du jour and have some fun trying to create a circumstance that is better than the one they're currently in. When we choose to be free from others' emotional grip, we gain the stability to contend with just about anyone's mood, no matter what the circumstance. It provides the space for us to think clearly, respond appropriately, innovate relevantly, and impact a life positively instead of being caught up in someone's negativity. We'll never be able to avoid being a target of dysfunction, since dysfunction is so pervasive, so it is best to be equipped to impact it and potentially bring healing to it. There is something quite satisfying when you can bring someone who is in pain to a place of peace or levity.

Consider the opportunity to be had in getting someone's number today!

- *What are the circumstances in which I allow people to get my number?*
- *If others treat me like a number, will I just give in, or will I step in and step up my game?*

Things done "on the side" are halfway on their way to being upside down.

Fragmented effort doesn't go a long way. It goes the wrong way! Since the economy has gone global, and connectivity makes anywhere in the world seem like next door, competition has reached heights of intensity that are flat-out fierce. The demand for focus and exemplary execution on everything is now considered "entry level," and if you want something to mature and be successful, going beyond *good enough* is mission critical. Seems everything in production these days is good enough, which means differentiation now and in the future will only be found in the "extraordinary." But this requires a focus that is equally extraordinary. I happen to believe that if you want to kill an important goal in life, add another goal into the mix, then another, and another. Before you know it, you'll have a bunch of fragmented goals, and with each unfinished project, your confidence and capacity to achieve the next one will diminish.

These days it's so easy to be distracted and so difficult to stay focused on the things that need the bulk of our attention. Yet the path of least resistance, most profitability, and greatest personal reward often rests in doing fewer things at a world-class level than many things at a no-class level. Fact is, it reflects poorly on our performance and our personal brand when we spread ourselves too thin.

Focus on the critical today.

- Do I have an inclination to be involved in too many things?
- Of the things I have in play, which ones should I bring to extraordinary, and which ones should I leave behind?

Do you spend more time talking yourself *into* doing good things or talking yourself *out* of doing them?

I'm convinced that we can convince ourselves convincingly into anything that is convincing.

We've covered the conversations we have with ourselves, but more specifically, the one conversation that has more impact than just about any other is found in the way in which we influence ourselves . . . or don't. We reason, rationalize, and justify our actions hundreds of times a day. We live in the bounce of "should I" or "shouldn't I" all day long, and we tend to spend more time talking ourselves *out of* doing positive things than talking ourselves *into* them.

The comfort revolution is at an all-time high. It started with the invention of the wheel, and ways to minimize our effort to accomplish haven't stopped since. Talking yourself out of things is nothing more than an investment of time—things like getting my spouse a card, calling my father to say hello, moving to a better position in business, reconciling that relationship. Could be a big thing or a small thing, but the decision *to do or not to do* is always looming.

Talking yourself into things is an investment of time as well— and usually a better one. Pushing past the illusion of comfort found in trepidation and saying yes to things rather than talking ourselves out of them creates a life filled with small to extraordinary surprises instead of a predictable drone of sameness and stuckness. The conversation we have with ourselves is nothing more than a habit of assaulting the voice that says, "I'll do it next time or get to it later." There is great enrichment to be had by taking the same time it takes to talk ourselves *out of* blessings and talking ourselves *into* them.

Start the habit of talking yourself into more things today.

- *What good things do I talk myself out of because it challenges my comfort?*
- *What could the habit of talking myself into things produce in my life?*

If you don't verbally and notably disagree with something, then consider yourself in agreement with it.

Silence is agreement. It's a form of lying down when you should be taking a stand.

Verbally disagreeing with something or someone can be an edgy proposition. *Not* disagreeing with someone you're in disagreement with is edgier . . . and riskier, due to the unknowns waiting ahead. For example, how many times has someone come to you and asked, "Is it done yet?" or "Did you get that thing?" only to have you respond with, "I never said I'd do that." And yet they insisted that you did. Perhaps the reason for the misunderstanding was because you said little or nothing to the contrary and were vague in the dialogue. Perhaps for the moment you went mute because you thought generalizations would do the trick instead of taking a stand, verbalizing your disagreement, and driving the point home that you *wouldn't* do what was requested of you.

When we don't take a verbal stand and disagree, then people will invent what they want about what it is they want. They're called assumptions, and they cause chaos when our stand to clearly disagree verbally and with conviction becomes DOA. The phrase for these voiceless agreements is *tacit agreements*, meaning semi-expressed, unsaid, or implied. The danger is that *implied* leaves the other thinking pretty much whatever they want about what you thought. There is great value in saying *no* to things in a way that is clear, or in disagreeing with things so it registers with others. In contrast to seeing this stand of clarity as an inconvenience to others, it should be embraced as an asset to them, as it lets them know in an instant where you *stand*, what you will *do*, what you will *not do*, and so on. It gives the gift of clarity to others and provides the gift of relational certainty back.

**Take a stand so that others
are clear about that stand today.**

- *Do people know where I stand, or do they act on what they think
I'm thinking?*
- *Does my strategy to avoid specificity cause more trouble
than it's worth?*

Rhythm is life-support to passion . . .

Keep the beat, keep your passion. Keep your vision in the groove!
If you've ever been on a dance floor, bustin' a smooth move,
and the music stops, you know what happens . . . or doesn't. Yeah, I
know, it probably took a little to get you out there in the first place,
and it probably took a bit to connect to the rhythm. But when the
beat stops, the feet stop, the hips freeze, the arms drop, and the
head . . . a sculpture.

Well, liken the word *passion* to the dance floor. When the beat of
passion skips due to distractions or a weak commitment, life slows,
progress freezes, interest drops, and we become dumbfounded, saying, "How did that happen? Where did my passion go?" Unlike a
person on the dance floor, the rhythm of passion is something that
doesn't suddenly stop, and it doesn't suddenly start, for that matter.
Excitement starts suddenly, but excitement should not be confused
with passion. Excitement is generally fleeting, where passion is a
building process that has a heartbeat . . . a rhythm. But the momentum of passion will begin to skip beats the moment we start to view
passion as an emotion more than a calling, a cause, and a vision. Feelings change but our passion shouldn't. Passion is a journey of getting
connected little by little through our efforts of qualification, implementation, measurement, refinement, and more implementation.

But consistency is key here. The times when the passion is under fire and in jeopardy is no time to slow the rhythm—adjust what we do, perhaps, or even the way that we do it, but keep the rhythm in play. It's that, or the internal tone that drives us and the passion that moves us will wane, and the music will eventually stop. Sound like a familiar song? It is—it's from a group called The Distractions, and the song is called "It's Over."

To ensure the passion lives, make sure the beat goes on today!

- *Are my goals in a rhythm, or do they need a pacemaker?*
- *What new things can I do to keep the vision alive and passion thriving?*

The victory in all arguments will come through key questions, not through manipulative statements.

Before you question who's at fault in the argument, ask some questions while in the argument.

We've covered arguments a bit in this book, because the next argument is en route. But again, arguments aren't bad. Stuffing resentment and unresolved issues? That's bad. In its purest form, an argument is nothing more than a revelation of what already exists between two or more people but hasn't been talked about until it reaches a boiling point. Then it becomes an argument, all because it wasn't dealt with early.

Unfortunately, two or more people bantering around statements in the height of emotion makes for a spectator sport more than it does progress. The destruction that takes place while emotions dominate over reason leaves a trail of hurt behind . . . nothing sporting about that.

A bit of awareness goes a long way to understanding how to gain power and control in a conflict, not to win it but to resolve it—responsibly. It's a little-known truth that as humans, it is difficult to be angry and curious at the same time—it's physiologically awkward. Moving to a curious disposition and into inquiry is where you'll end up after all the emotion subsides anyway. It begs the question, "Why not get curious at the first sign of trouble?" Asking questions provides answers and the openness to hear what's real rather than sifting through surface judgments and resentment. It's in the inquiry where we discover what is real, where we may have been at fault, and what is needed to facilitate understanding and reconciliation. Questions are the arsenal to kill the argument before the argument kills the relationship.

Think question marks before you communicate with damaging exclamation points today.

- *When an argument hits, will I become curious or become bitter?*
- *How much quicker would conflicts end if everyone inquired more and attacked less?*

Rawthenticity

The best city to live in is "authenti-*city*." Population? . . . Not enough!

Whoever that amazing person was who thought of the buzz-phrase "Keep it real" should have won the Pulitzer Prize. Shared in the right context, these three words are a driver for growth unlike any other. Although unpleasant for the time leading up to and at the moment, sharing truths with trusted others about our fears, problems, addictions, and concerns can be healing without the other offering up a single word of advice. Just the process of confessing the hard issues in our lives to trusted others has an uncanny ability to break the stronghold they have on us, and it clears our minds to think and talk through the issues with greater clarity with others.

I once shared a fear I'd been struggling with for most of my life. In fact, I was so ashamed of it, I had never told a single person, and I honestly never thought of sharing it with my wife. It was one of those "She'll certainly lose respect for me if I tell her" moments, and I thought, "Once it's out, it's out for good." So I dove in head-first and heart-first. I shared, I wept, and at the end of what I thought would be a total catastrophe, she simply said, "OK, we'll get some help with this." And I did. The strange thing is, not only was it freeing for me beyond my expectations, but my wife shared that she felt I was actually showing great strength and character by sharing it with her. And I got the added value of her unique way of supporting, praying, and encouraging me during the process of restoration. Everyone has their areas of breakdown in life . . . everyone. For us to think it unsafe to share is bigger than any breakdown we could ever have by becoming vulnerable with trusted others.

Consider sharing something that's been bottled up with someone you trust today.

- *What areas of life would I like some help with but am too prideful to ask?*
- *Who do I consider to be my trusted advisers in life, and are they underutilized?*

Consistency breeds refinement.
Refinement breeds more consistency.

Being better every day can be subverted by being different every day.

I love racquetball—it's a dynamic, fast-paced sport with more angles than a corrupt politician. Needless to say, like all midlife guys, I'm passionate about wanting to improve my play. So after another defeat by my racquetball partner, I took inventory of our games and I noticed that every time we play, I'm trying something new: new shots, angles, positions, and of course, new variations in trash talk—none of which were working, as I was still losing and my game was improving at a snail's pace. By taking inventory of my game, I was able to identify the shots that worked and the ones that didn't. The ironic thing was that none of my experimental shots made it to the shots-that-worked list. So I began to refine the five shots that were winners. I closed down the laboratory of shot making and began to refine the five key shots of my game. Not only did my shots improve, but I had more physical and mental energy to contend with the occasional surprises. I was calmer on the court, more clear thinking, and began to win more often.

There is something to be said for working on the winners by making ways to do those things that are proven and eliminating those things that aren't. So I looked at my career in the same light and found the same "disease." I was doing a lot of experimentation and getting poor results. After a bit of scrutiny, I realized there are four to five things I do really well. In fact, I'm deadly in these areas and at the top of my game. They give me energy and produce results, and I love doing them. So why chase after alternatives to success? Perhaps the repetitiveness got to me a bit, but when I realized I could bring a new vision of refinement to what was already working, life instantly started working better.

Close down the laboratory of uncertainty today. Work on your winners.

- *Do I value the adrenaline rush of experimentation over tried-and-true results?*
- *What are my sweet spots, the areas where my value screams progress?*

Difficult people are not a problem, they are a provision.

We all desire to grow in life. In fact, if I were to offer you the immediate ability to be more aware, insightful, approachable, adaptable, patient, and resilient, and to be a better communicator and listener, you'd probably ask, "How much?" I'd tell you it's available for the price of some minor initial discomfort and the acceptance that embracing difficult people is part of the bargain.

Unfortunately, our first instinct when we encounter people we don't gel with is to bolt. We discard them as offering no enjoyment or relevancy to our life. All probably true at first glance. But if you lean in a bit, you'll discover that difficult people present an opportunity to practice new ways of being with new kinds of people that will forge you into a stronger person while expanding your relatability, likability, social ability, conversational agility, overall civility, and sense of nobility so you can reduce future irritability. (Sorry!)

Difficult people are here to stay, so it makes sense to have the tools to deal with them in our mental arsenal. We get to sharpen our skills and become better-equipped to deal with every insecure, manipulative, arrogant, lazy, self-righteous, lackluster, idiotic person we meet. And we get to practice ways to move them into a way of being that is palatable, perhaps even enjoyable. The good news is that if you succeed, you'll have breathed life into despair and perhaps gained an ally. If you fail, you can shake it off and go again if you have the chance. Regardless, with every success or defeat, you'll improve your odds of emotional and social control while making human nature a little easier to contend with.

Don't avoid difficult people.
You have a toolbox, consider using it!

- *Do I typically avoid difficult people? Am I a difficult person myself?*
- *Can I see people who rub me wrong as an opportunity to do right?*

The price you pay often depends on the costs you count.

If you have a tendency toward complacency, it's best to consider what the future holds . . . *now*.

You can avoid unnecessary problems in the future when you take uninterrupted time to count the costs of your lack of action *now*. And when I say count the costs, I mean really evaluate what is actually going to happen if you continue placing more importance on convenience vs. commitment. Play out what non-action looks like and what it will mean all the way out to the end. Non-action always has an end—generally not a good one and usually nearer or worse than we imagine.

Whether in our marriage, career, relationships, or other areas that may be in peril, it seems the norm to do a razor-thin dig on the ramifications of what complacency will mean in these areas. We tend to glaze over the surface of these life-impacting issues only to get distracted before any real awareness of what is coming can take root. For some reason, people would rather pay the price of ignoring the issues than take the time to evaluate the cost, the loss, the pain, and the stress if things really go sideways. We fail to invite these thoughts in for a bit so we can feel in advance what it will be like, how life will be interrupted, what loss will entail, and how we and others will be affected if we don't combat comfort and get off the lazy train. There are areas in your life that need serious attention. These things (like cavities) will not fix themselves but will just get worse, and eventually will have to be dealt with at greater cost and pain. Consider that a bit of deep thought about these things will bring great revelation. Deep revelation will keep you out of deep . . .

Count the costs of what things will look like if you don't step up to the plate today.

- *Will I take time to count the costs of my current pace and commitments in life?*
- *What areas need immediate attention, and do I need help to get them on track?*

I think it's time I become extraordinarily me.

To be a poser or not to be a poser, that is the question. Fakespeare. Ever find yourself becoming someone other than the true you, just so you can feel accepted? The battle to just *be* is one that is tested at every turn of life. Every circumstance, conversation, and event is an opportunity to be either inauthentic or fully ourselves, without reserve, filter, or façade. So rather than spend mental energy and stress trying to fit the mold, bill, or circumstances, we can let our shoulders down, forgo the spotlight of performance, and just relax into ourselves—which, by the way, is nearly effortless.

I missed out on that effortlessness during my young adult life and into my early adult life because I was busy manufacturing whatever image I needed to look right, say it right, do it right, be accepted, and just deal with whatever circumstances needed from me. I mentioned in an earlier ShiftPoint that at one point, I told my wife, "I've got so many façades, I can't keep them straight." When she prompted me to share with my close friends and confess these façades, what she was saying was that by sharing these absolute truths with a trusted few (as scary as it sounded), it would begin the process of stripping me of my façades, and they would begin to disappear . . . and they did. The more honest I became, the more power they lost.

I discovered in this process that the level of our vulnerability to share from a place of total transparency will be proportional to the removal of façades, and the freedom to just be extraordinarily us will reveal itself. In contrast, the danger in keeping up any desired image is that without being fully ourselves, we never quite get to make the fine adjustments, because we are always adjusting the image—the plastic—and that, in and of itself, is a full-time job.

**Be extraordinarily you today,
without reserve or pretense.**

- *How much energy do I use keeping up my image? How's it working?*
- *Do I know what being fully me looks like? If not, am I willing to give it a try?*

If you want to fast-track your progress, stay perfectly still.

The discipline of stillness can be rocket fuel to growth.

It's ironic that we start out life waiting in one place for nine months, only to be in a frantic hurry for the rest of our lives. We think that by moving faster, thinking faster, acting faster, and being faster, things will happen faster. For today's sojourner, slow is the new fast, calm is the new force, and peace is the new profitability. In contrast to a twisted worldview, stillness doesn't mean stuckness—it actually means progress. Taking time to meditate and think through things thoroughly will create speed, efficiency, and better outcomes in all areas of life. It's like getting a steady stream of directional life signs, such as: rough road ahead, bridge out, dead-end street, yield, slow, stop, go, proceed with caution, and of course, a tribute to our humanness . . . dip ahead.

Ultimately, we avoid the crashes of life and get to our destinations quicker and with less stress if we're in touch with these signs, often found only in stillness. The commitment to be at rest for a moment and engage in stillness can occur anytime, anyplace. After a bit of practice, it only takes a short time to get to that amazing restful spot where innovation is found, solutions become clear, and the right choices become apparent. It only takes a couple of minutes to save hours, days, months, and years of wasting time cleaning up messes, rerouting our course, redoing what went wrong, and making up for missed innovations.

Quiet time? Try it sometime today.

- *When was the last time I slowed down to really think through my life?*
- *When would be good times of the day to experience the value of stillness?*

If we leave our health to its own devices, we will soon wind up on medical devices.

It shouldn't take a good health scare to drive us to good health care. The effects of poor health are quite subversive, meaning they don't show up until the doctor says, "You have diabetes," or "You have cancer," or "We don't know what it is, but it's serious." By this time, it's often too late. Doctor visits, surgical procedures, and hospital stays are just around the corner. Add to that, a leading cause of death in this country is complications from hospital visits, and letting our health get out of control can be a pretty scary thing, and it should be.

So let's hit the pause button today. Right now, in this moment, the most dependable, predictable health care system in the world consists of you, your mouth, and your commitment to exercise on a regular basis. It's a commitment that may not *eliminate* serious health issues, but it may *minimize* or prevent them. Aside from heredity, contracted disease, and rare cases, infection, disease, chronic conditions, even depression can be minimized or eliminated given the right food *intake* and exercise *output*. It's debatable, I know, but until the world, with its severe obesity rate, commits to healthy diet and exercise disciplines, it will be largely dependent on the health care system. It is estimated that in the next ten years, the obesity rate will jump even higher, and the burden this will have on individual health and wellness, the health care system, and the overall productivity of our nation will be tragic. Not to mention the pain and anguish our poor health will have on those who are forced to care for us. Tough words, yes, even for me, who could stand to lose a few pounds.

Consider the trajectory of your diet.
Contemplate what it will be like if you continue.

- *Is your diet leading you to the inevitable—early disease or premature death?*
- *Will I test run diet and exercise for thirty days to see what's in that momentum?*

That which you give your mind to will consume you . . . good or bad!
Moves Everyone Directly Into Anxiety.*

After a close friend went on a twenty-minute tirade about all the bad news in the world, I gently voiced the above headline, "That which you give your mind to will consume you . . . good or bad." I didn't have to share much beyond that, because he was so absorbed in the rhetoric of much of the media's perspectives that he was ready to be hit in the head with some candid, unbiased feedback. I also shared about an organization that inducts new members with a mandate to refrain from all TV, radio, and other media for thirty days, simply so they can hear things other than what the world is saying. They believe that reduction of media noise pays dividends of peace, perspective, and progress that can't be attained any other way.

I concur. Most (not all) mainstream media has discovered that producing conflict, anxiety, confusion, and fear raises ratings, and getting pulled into it is as easy as grabbing the remote. Flip through most of the channels, and you'll find a war of perspectives and sensationalism rooted partially in the facts, filtered mostly through personal biases, and steeled in personal agenda. It's enough to stress a corpse. It's a drip system of mental poison that can slowly kill the potential of who we can be . . . and it's extremely effective if we allow it to own a part of our lives. I'm not saying we should bury our head in the sand. There are responsible media outlets that are devoid of sensationalism and agenda where we can acquire the news we desire, and we should flag those as our sources. Whether from the media or people, it is critical to note that intake equals output affecting emotions, motivation, relationships, and our attitude and outlook on life.

Be cognizant of the news, views, and whatever you choose today.

• *Are the media making me feel needier and is the news giving me the blues?*
• *Will I use only responsible sources of media and govern my intake appropriately?*

*I cannot lump all media into this statement, nor is all media manipulative. I'll let you decide for yourself.

Experience the journey of journaling.

If you want life to be more *up*, write life *down*.

I've been encouraged to journal before but frankly never saw the value in it . . . until I started writing this book. It has been more or less an outlet for my experiences, insecurities, struggles, idiosyncrasies, problems, fears, challenges, realities . . . and I could go on for days. Yes, there are plenty of breakthroughs in the mix, but the value I've discovered in the process of journaling makes it a discipline I wish I had started decades ago. I don't know all the inherent value yet, but in the short time I have been writing down my thoughts, much of what I've considered to be true has become "absolute truth," driving new levels of awareness and progress that are nothing short of miraculous. It's as though with every page I type, a chapter of my past, present, or future life is clarified and put into a perspective that has me thinking fewer old, redundant thoughts and living more life—who woulda thought? The value of journaling places it somewhere between *thinking* about something and actually *experiencing* something. It's a cognitive exercise of processing life that etches what we write deeper into our experiences, our memory, and our conscious mind. It has a way of taking valuable thoughts we dabble with and making them part of who we are with intense conviction and resolve. Think it. Ink it. Reap it. Keep it. Yeah, that'll work.

Journal about today sometime before the end of the day.

- *Will I give journaling a try, even if only for five minutes a day?*
- *What is going on in my life that could use clarification and processing?*

One way or the other, you're always making a difference.

One can never say, "I'm not making a difference."

About twenty years ago, I was having lunch with a friend of mine (a mentor type), and he asked me (with that sinister look he always had) what I wanted to do with my life. I remember telling him that I wanted to make a difference with people. He said, "Well, Dean, good or bad, you're always making a difference." It sizzled my brain a bit, but he was right. Sometimes I was making a positive difference, other times the difference was pretty ugly. Yet things were always somehow different after my positive actions, negative actions, and even lack of action; impact never stopped.

I shared earlier that we were born to create and to generate, but also we were born to make a difference, meaning we cannot go a month, a week, or a day without making some kind of difference . . . good or bad. Forgive the extreme nature of the analogy, but Charles Manson made a difference, Hitler made a difference, Osama Bin Laden made a difference, just as Thomas Edison, Abraham Lincoln, and Mother Teresa made a difference. The difference is the kinds of impact that were made, but make no mistake about it, big differences were made on all accounts.

But also keep in mind that even Tom, Abe, and Teresa made differences that were less than what they committed to because they were human, and they would admit that. Why? Because they knew that truth makes a positive difference, and difference birthed in reality was primary for them.

Now that it's clear we are difference-making machines (with no *off* switch), the question becomes what kind of difference are you making in your life? Are you giving love or grief, providing serenity or anxiety, exposing positivity or skepticism, encouraging or distressing others, promoting unity or separatism, delivering honesty or deception? *All* differences, *all* happening 24/7, *all* opportunities one way or the other.

Make the kind of difference that grows, not slows things around you.

- *Are the differences I make improving life or degrading life?*
- *Are there new differences I'd like to integrate into my life?*

When making a difference to help others by sharing an individual ShiftPoint, it helps not to be shifty.

When handing out a single ShiftPoint to someone, use your judgment (discernment), not your judgment (indifference).

In the introduction of this book, I mentioned briefly that you might read a ShiftPoint that you feel would be beneficial to others—a topic or issue someone has been struggling with, or a current circumstance where a shift could cause a breakthrough or simply help move matters in the right direction. There's about a 100 percent chance of your discovering points that apply to others as I cover most categories of life. But we don't always have blanket permission to speak into others' lives, nor might the relationship be stable or strong enough for us to just be handing them out without thoughtful consideration. In fact, there are times I go to great lengths to tee up giving away a ShiftPoint to someone else because I don't want them to feel they're being judged. I also want them to clearly know the intentions of my heart are to serve and provide perspective, not condemn them. This is critical and may require some forethought on how best to approach this. A small investment of time and sensitivity should reap the relational dividends of a single ShiftPoint being well received. We cover both risk and sensitivity in this book, and when sharing feedback with others in any form, they go hand in hand. That said, I believe you will use your best judgment when sharing ShiftPoints with others. Happy shifting!

Give ample consideration when providing feedback, information, or resources to others.

- *When I give others feedback, will I take the time to tee it up well?*
- *Will I check in after the fact to see how things are going?*

Dean Del Sesto has been in the marketing, branding, and business development sectors his whole life. From selling mismarked candy at school at age eleven, to selling avocados on a street corner at fourteen, to eventually cofounding and building one of the largest ad agencies in Orange County, California, he has always loved the creative field. Today, he runs an award-winning branding, interactive, and communications agency located in Laguna Beach, California, called Breviti (www.breviti.com) and is also a partner at Veracity Colab, a B2B and consumer video marketing agency in Newport Beach, California (www.veracity colab.com). With over twenty-five years in the field, Dean has had the pleasure to be directly involved in the local- to enterprise-wide brand development of over eight hundred companies and *still* loves it today!

As for community involvement, Dean finds great joy in counseling, advising, and collaborating with others in the areas of marriage, relationships, business, and life problem solving.

Dean and his wife have been married over twenty years, live in Laguna Beach, and are involved with multiple nonprofit organizations in a variety of categories.

DEAN DEL SESTO.COM
BUILD YOUR BRAND ONE SHIFT AT A TIME

"After creating over 800 brands, I've come to learn it's
'STAND OUT OR BE COUNTED OUT.'
Every move, action, strategy, tactic, and detail will
position you to be either selected or rejected depending
on the resonance and relevance of your brand." —dds

For all things branding, visit
DEANDELSESTO.COM to learn

- How the world of branding has changed & why you must adapt
- Ways to build & maintain a brand that demands attention
- The importance of both personal & corporate brand disciplines
- Marketing strategies & tactics that make sense & make money
- How your brand affects relationships & improves your influence

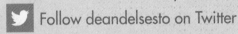 Follow deandelsesto on Twitter

for brief original quotes that will help you grow, shift,
smile, and yes . . . even laugh now and then!